AMERICA'S HEALTHY COOKING

desserts

AMERICA'S HEALTHY COOKING

desserts

JG
PRESS

Published by World Publications Group, Inc.
455 Somerset Avenue
North Dighton, MA 02764
www.wrldpub.net

All photographs courtesy of Sunset Books

ISBN 1-57215-419-5

Editors: Joel Carino and Emily Zelner
Designer: Lynne Yeamans/Lync
Production Director: Ellen Milionis

Printed and bound in China by SNP Leefung Printers Limited.

1 2 3 4 5   06 05 03 02

desserts

apple-fennel tart

preparation time: 30 minutes
cooking time: about 1¼ hours

¹/₂ **cup dried currants**

³/₄ **cup plus 2 teaspoons all-purpose flour**

¹/₂ **cup regular rolled oats**

¹/₄ **cup butter or margarine, cut into chunks**

1 large egg white

¹/₃ **cup granulated sugar**

1 teaspoon ground cinnamon

2 cups sliced apples such as Newtown Pippin (cut slices ¹/₄ inch thick)

1¹/₂ cups sliced fennel (cut slices ¹/₄ inch thick)

2 teaspoons lemon juice

About 2 tablespoons sifted powdered sugar

1 Place currants in a small bowl and add enough water to cover. Let stand until currants are softened (about 10 minutes), stirring occasionally. Drain well; set aside.

2 In a food processor, combine ³/₄ cup of the flour, oats, and butter. Whirl until mixture resembles fine crumbs. Add egg white; whirl until dough holds together. Press dough evenly over bottom and sides of an 8-inch tart pan with a removable rim.

3 In a large bowl, mix remaining 2 teaspoons flour, granulated sugar, cinnamon, and currants. Add apples, fennel, and lemon juice; mix well. Pour fruit mixture into pan; pat to make level.

4 Bake on lowest rack of a 425° oven until top of filling begins to brown (about 45 minutes). Drape tart with foil; continue to bake until juices begin to bubble (about 30 more minutes).

5 Remove pan rim; slide a wide spatula under hot tart to release crust (leave tart in place). Serve warm or cool; dust with powdered sugar before serving.

makes 6 servings

per serving: 268 calories, 4 g protein, 46 g carbohydrates, 8 g total fat, 21 mg cholesterol, 116 mg sodium

cherry apple jubilee

preparation time: about 25 minutes

¹/₂ **cup dried pitted cherries or raisins**

2 tablespoons brandy

About 1 tablespoon kirsch

3 large Golden Delicious apples

1 tablespoon lemon juice

¹/₃ **cup firmly packed brown sugar**

2 cups vanilla nonfat frozen yogurt

Mint sprigs

1 In a small bowl, combine cherries, brandy, and 1 tablespoon of the kirsch; let stand until cherries are softened (about 10 minutes), stirring occasionally.

2 Meanwhile, peel and core apples; then cut into ¹/₄- to ¹/₂-inch-thick slices. Place in a large bowl, add lemon juice, and mix gently to coat. Set aside.

3 In a wide nonstick frying pan or wok, combine sugar and 2 tablespoons water. Add apples; stir-fry gently over medium-high heat until apples are almost tender when pierced (4 to 5 minutes). Add cherries (and any soaking liquid) and stir just until heated through.

4 Divide fruit mixture among 4 individual bowls; top equally with frozen yogurt. Garnish with mint sprigs. Offer additional kirsch to drizzle over yogurt, if desired.

makes 4 servings

per serving: 323 calorie, 2 g protein, 74 g carbohydrates, 0.5 g total fat, 0 mg cholesterol, 53 mg sodium

cream cheese blond brownies

preparation time: about 40 minutes

1 large package (about 8 oz.) nonfat
   cream cheese, at room temperature

1/2 cup granulated sugar

2 large egg whites

1/4 cup nonfat sour cream

1 1/4 cups plus 1 tablespoon all-purpose flour

1 tablespoon vanilla

1 teaspoon baking powder

1/4 cup chopped walnuts

1/3 cup pure maple syrup

1/3 cup firmly packed brown sugar

1/3 cup butter or margarine,
   at room temperature

1 large egg

1. In a small bowl, combine cream cheese, granulated sugar, egg whites, sour cream, 1 tablespoon of the flour, and 1 teaspoon of the vanilla. Beat until smooth; set aside. In another small bowl, stir together remaining 1 1/4 cups flour, baking powder, and walnuts; set aside.

2. In a large bowl, combine syrup, brown sugar, butter, egg, and remaining 2 teaspoons vanilla. Beat until smooth. Add flour mixture; beat until dry ingredients are evenly moistened.

3. Pour two-thirds of the brownie batter into a lightly greased 8-inch-square nonstick or regular baking pan; spread to make level. Pour cheese mixture evenly over batter. Drop remaining batter by spoonfuls over cheese mixture; swirl with a knife to blend batter slightly with cheese mixture.

4. Bake in a 350° oven until a wooden pick inserted in center comes out clean (about 25 minutes; pierce brownie, not cheese mixture). Let cool in pan on a rack, then cut into 2-inch squares.

makes 16 brownies

per brownie: 168 calories, 4 g protein, 25 g carbohydrates, 6 g total fat, 25 mg cholesterol, 153 mg sodium

ginger bars

preparation time: 35 to 40 minutes

1 cup whole wheat flour

1/4 cup sugar

1/2 teaspoon baking soda

3 tablespoons coarsely chopped crystallized or
   candied ginger

1/4 cup nonfat milk

1/4 cup molasses

2 large egg whites

1. In a large bowl, stir together flour, sugar, baking soda, and ginger. Add milk, molasses, and egg whites; beat until smoothly blended.

2. Spread batter evenly in a lightly greased 8-inch-square nonstick or regular baking pan. Bake in a 350° oven until center springs back when lightly pressed (20 to 25 minutes). Serve warm or cool; to serve, cut into 2-inch squares. These bars are best eaten fresh, so serve them the same day you make them.

makes 16 bars

per bar: 67 calories, 2 g protein, 15 g carbohydrates, 0.4 g total fat, 0.1 mg cholesterol, 52 mg sodium

molasses sugar cookies

preparation time: about 30 minutes

2 cups all-purpose flour

1 1/2 teaspoons baking powder

1 teaspoon ground ginger

1 teaspoon ground cinnamon

1/2 teaspoon salt

1/4 teaspoon baking soda

1/2 cup butter or margarine,
   at room temperature

1/2 cup firmly packed brown sugar

2 large egg whites

1/2 cup molasses

2 teaspoons instant espresso powder
   or coffee powder

About 2/3 cup sugar cubes, coarsely crushed

About 1/4 cup granulated sugar

1 In a medium-size bowl, stir together flour, baking powder, ginger, cinnamon, salt, and baking soda; set aside.

2 In a food processor or a large bowl, combine butter, brown sugar, egg whites, molasses, instant espresso powder, and 1/2 cup water. Whirl or beat with an electric mixer until smooth. Add flour mixture to butter mixture; whirl or beat until dry ingredients are evenly moistened.

3 Spoon rounded 1-tablespoon portions of dough onto lightly greased large nonstick or regular baking sheets, spacing cookies about 2 inches apart.

4 Bake in a 350° oven for 5 minutes. Remove from oven. Working quickly, sprinkle each cookie with about 3/4 teaspoon of the crushed sugar cubes; press in lightly. Return cookies to oven and bake until firm to the touch (about 2 more minutes). Let cookies cool on baking sheets for about 3 minutes. Transfer to racks, sprinkle with granulated sugar, and cool completely.

makes about 3 dozen cookies

per cookie: 93 calories, 0.9 g protein, 17 g carbohydrates, 3 g total fat, 7 mg cholesterol, 91 mg sodium

cherry chimichangas

preparation time: about 25 minutes

2 teaspoons berry-flavored liqueur

1 or 2 teaspoons cornstarch

1/4 cup cherry preserves

1 teaspoon grated lemon peel

2 cups pitted, chopped fresh cherries,
   or 2 cups frozen pitted dark sweet cherries,
   thawed, chopped, and drained well

6 flour tortillas

About 1/3 cup nonfat milk

Powdered sugar

1 In a bowl, combine liqueur and cornstarch until smooth (use 1 teaspoon cornstarch if using fresh cherries; use 2 teaspoons cornstarch mixed with 2 teaspoons water if using thawed frozen cherries). Stir in preserves, lemon peel, and cherries.

2 To assemble each chimichanga, brush both sides of a tortilla liberally with milk; let stand briefly to soften tortilla. Place a sixth of the filling on tortilla. Lap ends of tortilla over filling; then fold sides to center to make a packet. Place chimichanga, seam side down, on a lightly oiled 12- by 15-inch baking sheet; brush with milk. Repeat to make 5 more chimichangas.

3 Bake in a 500° oven, brushing with milk twice, until golden brown (8 to 10 minutes). Cool slightly, dust with sugar, and serve warm.

makes 6 chimichangas

per chimichanga: 203 calories, 4 g protein, 40 g carbohydrates, 3 g total fat, 0.3 mg cholesterol, 180 mg sodium

orange pudding parfaits

preparation time: about 35 minutes
chilling time: about 4 hours

3 tablespoons quick-cooking tapioca

$^1/_3$ cup sugar

2 egg whites

2 $^1/_2$ cups nonfat milk

$^1/_2$ teaspoon vanilla

1 tablespoon *each* grated orange peel
and orange-flavored liqueur

2 large oranges

1 In a 2- to 3-quart pan, stir together tapioca, sugar, egg whites, and milk; let stand for 5 minutes. Then bring to a full boil over medium heat, stirring constantly. Remove from heat and stir in vanilla, orange peel, and liqueur. Let cool, uncovered, stirring once after 20 minutes.

2 Using a sharp knife, cut peel and all white membrane from oranges; cut segments free and lift out. Layer cooled tapioca and orange segments in four 8-ounce parfait glasses. Cover and refrigerate until cold before serving (about 4 hours).

makes 4 servings

per serving: 189 calories, 8 g protein, 40 g carbohydrates, 0.4 g total fat, 3 mg cholesterol, 105 mg sodium

bananas with pound cake & chocolate sauce

preparation time: about 25 minutes

$^1/_2$ cup firmly packed brown sugar

$^1/_4$ cup unsweetened cocoa powder

1 tablespoon cornstarch

$^1/_4$ teaspoon instant coffee powder

$^1/_2$ cup water

2 tablespoons light corn syrup

2 teaspoons light or dark rum, or to taste

$^1/_2$ teaspoon vanilla

3 large bananas

1 tablespoon lemon juice

1 tablespoon sweetened shredded coconut

3 tablespoons granulated sugar

4 slices purchased nonfat pound cake,
each about $^3/_4$ inch thick

1 To prepare chocolate sauce, in a small pan, combine brown sugar, cocoa, cornstarch, and coffee powder. Add water and corn syrup; stir until smooth. Cook over medium-high heat, stirring until mixture boils and thickens slightly, about 4 minutes. (At this point, you may cover to prevent a film from forming on top, let cool, and refrigerate for up to 3 days.) If preparing ahead, reheat, stirring, before adding rum and vanilla. Otherwise, remove pan from heat and stir in rum and vanilla immediately. Keep warm, stirring occasionally.

2 Cut bananas diagonally into $^1/_2$-inch-thick slices; place in a large bowl, add lemon juice, and mix gently to coat. Set aside.

3 In a wide nonstick frying pan or wok, stir coconut over medium heat until golden (about 3 minutes). Remove from pan and set aside. To pan, add granulated sugar and 2 tablespoons water. Cook over medium-high heat, stirring, until sugar is dissolved. Add bananas; stir-fry gently until bananas are hot and sauce is thick and bubbly (about 2 minutes). Remove from heat.

4 Place one slice of cake on each of 4 individual plates; spoon banana mixture over cake. Just before serving, stir chocolate sauce well. Drizzle cake with sauce and sprinkle with coconut.

makes 4 servings

per serving: 410 caloriess, 4 g protein, 100 g carbohydrates, 2 g total fat, 0 mg cholesterol, 225 mg sodium

lemon poppy seed cake

preparation time: about 45 minutes

3 large eggs

2 large egg white

1 cup granulated sugar

1/2 cup smooth unsweetened applesauce

1 1/2 cups all-purpose flour

1/4 cup poppy seeds

1 tablespoons baking powder

1 tablespoon plus 1 teaspoon grated lemon peel

1/2 cup butter or margarine, melted, plus 1/3 cup
   butter or margarine, at room temperature

3 cups powdered sugar

1/2 cup nonfat sour cream

2/3 cup strawberry jam

Thin strips of lemon peel

About 8 cups fresh strawberries,
   hulled and halved

1 In a food processor or a large bowl, combine eggs, egg whites, granulated sugar, and applesauce; whirl or beat with an electric mixer until mixture is thick and lemon-colored. Add flour, poppy seeds, baking powder, 1 tablespoon of the grated lemon peel, and the 1/2 cup melted butter; whirl or beat until dry ingredients are evenly moistened. Divide batter equally between 2 greased, floured 8-inch-round nonstick or regular baking pans.

2 Bake in a 375° oven until cake layers just begin to pull away from sides of pans and centers spring back when gently pressed (about 15 minutes); halfway through baking, gently rotate each pan one-half turn. Let cakes cool for 10 minutes in pans on racks; then turn out of pans to cool completely.

3 Meanwhile, prepare frosting: In clean food processor or large bowl, combine powdered sugar, sour cream, the 1/3 cup butter at room temperature, and remaining 1 teaspoon grated lemon peel. Whirl or beat with electric mixer until frosting is smooth and spreadable; cover and refrigerate until ready to use.

4 To assemble cake, brush all loose crumbs from sides and bottom of each cake layer. Center one layer, top side down, on a serving plate. Using a metal spatula, evenly spread jam to within 1/2 inch of edge. Top with second layer, top side up.

5 Stir frosting and spread over sides and top of cake; arrange strips of lemon peel decoratively atop cake. To serve, cut cake into slices; offer strawberries alongside.

makes 10 to 12 servings

per serving: 528 calories, 6 g protein, 88 g carbohydrates, 18 g total fat, 95 mg cholesterol, 319 mg sodium

stir-fried pineapple with ginger

preparation time: about 15 minutes

1 tablespoon butter or margarine

5 cups 1/2-inch chunks fresh or canned pineapple

1/3 cup firmly packed brown sugar

1 tablespoon finely chopped crystallized ginger

1/4 teaspoon grated lime peel

1 tablespoon lime juice

1 1/3 cups coarsely crushed gingersnaps

Mint sprigs

1 Melt butter in a wide nonstick frying pan or wok over medium-high heat. Add pineapple, sugar, ginger, lime peel, and lime juice. Stir-fry gently until pineapple is heated through (about 5 minutes).

2 Transfer fruit and sauce to a shallow serving bowl; sprinkle with crushed gingersnaps. Garnish with mint sprigs.

makes 4 servings

per serving: 291 calories, 2 g protein, 62 g carbohydrates, 6 g total fat, 8 mg cholesterol, 178 mg sodium

chocolate chip cookies

preparation time: about 35 minutes

1 1/2 cups all-purpose flour

1 teaspoon baking powder

1/2 teaspoon baking soda

1/2 teaspoon salt

2 tablespoons butter or margarine,
    at room temperature

2 tablespoons vegetable oil

1 cup firmly packed dark brown sugar

1 large egg

1/2 cup smooth unsweetened applesauce

1 teaspoon vanilla

2 cups regular rolled oats

1 package (about 6 oz.) semisweet
    chocolate chips

About 2 tablespoons granulated sugar

1 In a medium-size bowl, stir together flour, baking powder, baking soda, and salt; set aside.

2 In a large bowl, beat butter, oil, and brown sugar with an electric mixer until smooth. Add egg, applesauce, and vanilla; beat until blended. Add flour mixture and beat until smooth. Scrape down sides of bowl; stir in oats and chocolate chips.

3 Shape and bake dough right away; if it is allowed to sit, cookies will be dry. Working quickly, spoon 2-tablespoon portions of dough onto lightly greased large nonstick or regular baking sheets, spacing cookies evenly. Dip fingertips in granulated sugar, then pat cookies into rounds about 1/3 inch thick.

4 Bake in a 350° oven until pale golden (about 10 minutes), switching positions of baking sheets halfway through baking. Let cool for about 3 minutes on baking sheets, then transfer to racks to cool completely. Serve warm or cool.

makes about 2 dozen cookies

per cookie: 154 calories, 2 g protein, 26 g carbohydrates, 5 g total fat, 11 mg cholesterol, 109 mg sodium

frosted corinth grapes

preparation time: about 20 minutes
chilling time: about 3 hours

4 clusters (about 1 1/2 lbs. *total*) Black Corinth
    grapes (also called champagne grapes), rinsed

1 egg white, lightly beaten

3/4 cup sugar

Lemon sorbet (optional)

1 Lay clusters of grapes flat. Turning fruit with stem, gently brush all over with egg white. With a helper holding each cluster horizontally by stem and fruit ends, sprinkle with sugar, having helper turn fruit as you work.

2 Clip stems with a clothespin to a wrack in freezer, being sure nothing touches grapes (put plastic wrap beneath to catch any drips). Freeze until solid (about 3 hours) If made ahead, seal in a plastic bag and freeze for up to 2 months.

3 Offer with sorbet, if desired.

makes 4 servings

per serving: 247 calories, 2 g protein, 64 g carbohydrates, 0.5 g total fat, 0 mg cholesterol, 17 mg sodium

cocoa pepper cookies

preparation time: about 45 minutes

1 cup all-purpose flour

2 tablespoons unsweetened cocoa powder

1 teaspoon baking powder

1 cup sugar

1 teaspoon whole black peppercorns, coarsely crushed

2 tablespoons butter, melted

1/3 cup smooth unsweetened applesauce

1/2 teaspoon vanilla

1 In a food processor (or in a bowl), combine flour, cocoa, baking powder, 3/4 cup of the sugar, and peppercorns. Whirl (or stir) until blended. Add butter, applesauce, and vanilla; whirl until dough forms a compact ball. (Or stir in butter, applesauce, and vanilla with a fork, then work dough with your hands to form a smooth-textured ball.)

2 With lightly floured fingers, pinch off 1-inch pieces of dough and roll into balls. Arrange balls 2 inches apart on two 12- by 15-inch nonstick (or lightly greased regular) baking sheets. Dip bottom of a lightly greased glass into remaining 1/4 cup sugar and press each ball gently to a thickness of about 1/2 inch; dip glass again as needed to prevent sticking.

3 Bake in lower third of a 300° oven until cookies are firm to the touch and look dry on top (about 20 minutes), switching positions of baking sheets halfway through baking. Let cookies cool on baking sheets for about 3 minutes; then transfer to racks to cool completely.

makes about 1 1/2 dozen cookies

per cookie: 84 calories, 0.7 g protein, 18 g carbohydrates, 1 g total fat, 3 mg cholesterol, 41 mg sodium

mexican wedding cookies

preparation time: about 40 minutes

1 1/2 cups all-purpose flour

1 teaspoon baking powder

1/4 teaspoon salt

5 tablespoons butter or margarine, at room temperature

1/3 cup unsweetened applesauce

About 1 1/2 cups powdered sugar

1 large egg

1 teaspoon vanilla

1/4 cup chopped pecans

1 In a small bowl, mix flour, baking powder, and salt. In a food processor (or in a large bowl), whirl (or beat) butter and applesauce until well blended. Add 1/2 cup of the sugar, egg, vanilla, and pecans; whirl (or beat) until smooth. Add flour mixture to egg mixture; whirl (or stir) until blended. Dough will be stiff.

2 With lightly floured fingers, shape 2-teaspoon portions of dough into balls; you should have 24. Set balls 1 inch apart on two 12- by 15-inch nonstick (or lightly greased regular) baking sheets. Bake in a 375° oven until cookies are light golden brown (about 15 minutes), switching positions of baking sheets halfway through baking. Let cool on baking sheets until lukewarm.

3 Sift 1/2 cup of the remaining sugar onto a large sheet of wax paper. Roll each cookie gently in sugar. With your fingers, pack more sugar all over each cookie to a depth of about 1/8 inch. Place cookies on a rack over wax paper and dust with remaining sugar; let cool.

makes 2 dozen cookies

per cookie: 84 calories, 1 g protein, 14 g carbohydrates, 2 g total fat, 13 mg cholesterol, 60 mg sodium

lemon cookies

preparation time: about 40 minutes

$1/2$ **cup all-purpose flour**

$1/4$ **teaspoon baking soda**

$1/4$ **teaspoon salt**

$1/8$ **teaspoon cream of tartar**

2 tablespoons butter or margarine, at room temperature

6 tablespoons granulated sugar

2 teaspoons lemon peel

2 $1/2$ teaspoons lemon juice

$1/2$ **teaspoon vanilla**

1 large egg white

$1/2$ **cup regular rolled oats**

$2/3$ **cup sifted powdered sugar**

1. In a small bowl, mix flour, baking soda, salt, and cream of tartar. In a food processor (or in a large bowl), whirl (or beat) butter, granulated sugar, lemon peel, $1/2$ teaspoon of the lemon juice, vanilla, and egg white until well blended. Add flour mixture to egg mixture; whirl (or stir) until combined. Stir in oats.

2. With floured fingers, divide dough into $1 1/2$-teaspoon portions (you should have 18); place mounds of dough 2 inches apart on two 12- by 15-inch nonstick (or lightly greased regular) baking sheets.

3. Bake in a 350°F oven until cookies are light golden and firm to the touch (about 15 minutes), switching positions of baking sheets halfway through baking. Let cookies cool on baking sheets for about 3 minutes; then transfer to racks to cool completely.

4. While cookies are baking, prepare lemon icing: In a small bowl, combine powdered sugar, remaining 2 teaspoons lemon juice, and water. Stir until smooth.

5. Set each rack of cookies over a baking sheet to catch any drips; drizzle icing evenly over cookies. Serve; or let stand until icing hardens.

makes $1 1/2$ dozen cookies

per cookie: 65 calories, 0.9 g protein, 12 g carbohydrates, 1 total fat, 3 mg cholesterol, 64 mg sodium

hot papaya sundaes

preparation time: about 30 minutes

1 tablespoon margarine, melted

$1/2$ **teaspoon grated lime peel**

$1/3$ **cup rum or water**

$1/4$ **cup lime juice**

3 tablespoons honey

2 small firm-ripe papayas

2 cups vanilla low-fat frozen yogurt

1. In a 9- by 13-inch casserole, stir together margarine, lime peel, rum, lime juice, and honey.

2. Cut unpeeled papayas in half lengthwise; scoop out and discard seeds, then place papaya halves, cut sides down, in honey mixture. Bake in a 375° oven until papayas are heated through and sauce is just beginning to bubble (about 15 minutes).

3. Carefully transfer hot papaya halves, cut sides up, to dessert plates; let stand for about 5 minutes.

4. Meanwhile, stir pan juices in casserole to blend; pour into a small pitcher. Fill each papaya half with small scoops of frozen yogurt; offer pan juices to pour over sundaes to taste.

makes 4 servings

per serving: 270 calories, 4 g protein, 46 g carbohydrates, 5 g total fat, 5 mg cholesterol, 101 mg sodium

chocolate pistachio cookies

preparation time: about 40 minutes

1 cup all-purpose flour

2 tablespoons unsweetened cocoa powder

1 teaspoon baking powder

1/4 teaspoon instant espresso or coffee powder

1 cup granulated sugar

2 tablespoons butter or margarine, melted

1/3 cup smooth unsweetened applesauce

1/2 teaspoon vanilla

1/4 cup shelled pistachio nuts, chopped

1/2 cup powdered sugar

1 In a food processor or a large bowl, whirl or stir together flour, cocoa, baking powder, instant espresso, and ³/4 cup of the granulated sugar. Add butter, applesauce, and vanilla; whirl until dough forms a compact ball. (Or, if not using a processor, stir in butter, applesauce, and vanilla with a fork, then work dough with your hands to form a smooth-textured ball.)

2 With lightly floured fingers, pinch off about 1-inch pieces of dough; roll pieces into balls. Set balls 2 inches apart on lightly greased large nonstick or regular baking sheets.

3 Place remaining ¹/4 cup granulated sugar in a shallow bowl. Dip bottom of a lightly greased glass in sugar; use glass to press each ball of dough gently to a thickness of about ¹/2 inch. After flattening each ball, dip glass in sugar again to prevent sticking. Sprinkle cookies evenly with pistachios.

4 Bake in lower third of a 300° oven until cookies are firm to the touch and look dry on top (about 20 minutes), switching positions of baking sheets halfway through baking.

5 Let cookies cool on baking sheets for about 3 minutes, then transfer to racks to cool completely. Meanwhile, in a small bowl, smoothly blend powdered sugar with 1¹/2 to 2 teaspoons water, or enough to make icing easy to drizzle. Drizzle icing over cooled cookies.

makes about 2 dozen cookies

per cookie: 83 calories, 0.9 g protein, 16 g carbohydrates, 2 g total fat, 3 mg cholesterol, 31 mg sodium

maple date bars

preparation time: 35 minutes

³/4 cup whole wheat flour

1/2 teaspoon each baking powder and baking soda

1/2 cup chopped pitted dates

1/2 cup pure maple syrup

2 large egg whites

1/2 teaspoon vanilla

1 In a large bowl, stir together flour, baking powder, baking soda, and dates. Add syrup, egg whites, and vanilla; beat until smooth.

2 Spread batter evenly in a lightly greased square 8-inch non-stick or regular baking pan. Bake in a 350° oven until center springs back when lightly pressed (about 20 minutes). Serve warm or cool; to serve, cut into 2-inch squares. These bars are best eaten fresh, so serve them the same day you make them.

makes 16 bars

per bar: 65 calories, 1 g protein, 15 g carbohydrates, 0.4 g total fat, 0 mg cholesterol, 62 mg sodium

espresso biscotti

preparation time: about 1 1/4 hours

1/2 cup hazelnuts

5 tablespoons butter or margarine,
    at room temperature

1/2 cup granulated sugar

2 1/2 teaspoons instant espresso powder

1 large egg

2 large egg whites

1 teaspoon vanilla

2 cups all-purpose flour

2 teaspoons baking powder

1 1/2 cups sifted powdered sugar

1 Spread hazelnuts in a single layer in a shallow baking pan. Bake in a 375° oven until nuts are golden beneath skins (about 10 minutes). Let nuts cool slightly; then pour into a towel and rub to remove as much loose skin as possible. Let cool; chop coarsely and set aside. Reduce oven temperature to 350°.

2 In a large bowl, beat butter, granulated sugar, and 1 1/2 teaspoons of the instant espresso until well blended. Add egg and egg whites, beating until well blended. Stir in vanilla. In a medium-size bowl, stir together flour and baking powder; add to butter mixture and stir until well blended. Mix in hazelnuts.

3 Divide dough in half. On a lightly floured board, shape each portion into a long roll about 1 1/2 inches in diameter. Place rolls on a large nonstick or greased regular baking sheet, 3 inches apart. Flatten rolls to make loaves 1/2-inch thick. Bake in a 350° oven until loaves feel firm to the touch (about 15 minutes).

4 Remove baking sheet from oven and let loaves cool for 3 to 5 minutes; then cut crosswise into slices about 1/2 inch thick. Tip slices cut side down on baking sheet (at this point, you may need another sheet to bake biscotti all at once). Return to oven and bake until biscotti look dry and are lightly browned (about 10 minutes); if using 2 baking sheets, switch their positions halfway through baking. Transfer biscotti to racks and let cool.

5 In a small bowl, dissolve remaining 1 teaspoon instant espresso in 4 teaspoons very hot water. Stir in powdered sugar; if needed, add more hot water, 1 teaspoon at a time, to make icing easy to spread.

6 Spread icing over 1 to 1 1/2 inches of one end of each cooled cookie. Let stand until icing is firm before serving.

makes about 4 dozen cookies

per cookie: 60 calories, 1 g protein, 10 g carbohydrates, 2 g total fat, 7 mg cholesterol, 35 mg sodium

espresso chocolate cake with orange sauce

preparation time: about 1 1/4 hours

2 tablespoons butter or margarine,
    at room temperature

1 cup firmly packed brown sugar

1 large egg

3 large egg whites

1 cup nonfat sour cream

1 teaspoon vanilla

3/4 cup all-purpose flour

1/3 cup unsweetened cocoa powder

1 tablespoon instant espresso powder

1 1/2 teaspoons baking powder

6 or 7 large oranges

6 tablespoons granulated sugar

4 teaspoons cornstarch

1 1/2 teaspoons instant espresso powder
    (or to taste)

1 1/2 cups fresh orange juice

2 tablespoons orange-flavored liqueur
    (or to taste)

2 tablespoons unsweetened cocoa powder

Mint sprigs

1. In a food processor or a large bowl, combine butter and brown sugar; whirl or beat with an electric mixer until well blended. Add egg, egg whites, sour cream, and vanilla; whirl or beat until well blended. Add flour, the 1/3 cup cocoa, the 1 tablespoon instant espresso, and baking powder; whirl or beat just until combined. Spread batter in a greased square 8-inch nonstick or regular baking pan. Bake in a 350° oven until cake begins to pull away from pan sides and center springs back when lightly pressed (35 to 40 minutes).

2. While cake is baking, finely shred enough peel (colored part only) from oranges to make 1 to 2 teaspoons for sauce; cover and set aside. Cut off and discard remaining peel and all white membrane from oranges. Cut between membranes to release segments. Cover orange segments and set aside.

3. In a small pan, combine granulated sugar, cornstarch, and the 1 1/2 teaspoons instant espresso. Whisk in orange juice and the reserved shredded orange peel; cook over medium-high heat, stirring constantly, until sauce boils and thickens slightly (about 1 minute). Remove from heat and stir in liqueur.

4. Just before serving, sift the 2 tablespoons cocoa over cake. Cut cake into diamonds, triangles, or squares; transfer to individual plates. Arrange orange segments alongside. Drizzle sauce over oranges. Garnish with mint sprigs. Makes 8 servings.

per serving: 361 calories, 8 g protein, 74 g carbohydrates, 5 g total fat, 34 mg cholesterol, 187 mg sodium

strawberries with gingered vanilla yogurt

preparation time: about 1 1/4 hours

About 3/4 pound large strawberries
    with stems, rinsed and drained

3/4 cup vanilla lowfat yogurt

1/4 teaspoon ground ginger

Arrange berries on a serving platter. In a small bowl, stir together yogurt and ginger. Offer with berries for dipping.

makes 2 servings

per serving: 121 calories, 5 g protein, 23 g carbohydrates, 2 g total fat, 4 mg cholesterol, 58 mg sodium

espresso cheesecake

preparation time: 25 minutes
cooking time: 1¹/₂ to 1³/₄ hours
cooling and chilling time: at least 4¹/₂ hours

1 package (about 9 oz.) chocolate
    wafer cookies

¹/₄ cup butter or margarine,
    melted and cooled slightly

1 tablespoon instant espresso powder

¹/₂ teaspoon vanilla

4 large packages (about 8 oz. *each*) nonfat
    cream cheese, at room temperature

1 cup sugar

3 large eggs

2 large egg whites

2 cups nonfat sour cream

3 tablespoons coffee-flavored liqueur

1 tablespoon sugar

1 tablespoon unsweetened cocoa powder

Chocolate-covered espresso beans
    or mocha candy beans

1 In a food processor, whirl cookies to form fine crumbs. Add butter, instant espresso, and vanilla; whirl just until crumbs are evenly moistened. Press crumb mixture firmly over bottom and about 1 inch up sides of a greased 9-inch cheesecake pan with a removable rim. Bake in a 350° oven until crust feels slightly firmer when pressed (about 15 minutes). In clean food processor or in a large bowl, combine cream cheese, the 1 cup sugar, eggs, egg whites, 1 cup of the sour cream, and liqueur. Whirl or beat with an electric mixer until smooth. Pour cheese filling into baked crust. Return to oven and bake until filling is golden on top and jiggles only slightly in center when pan is gently shaken (1¹/₄ to 1¹/₂ hours).

2 Gently run a slender knife between cheesecake and pan rim; then let cheesecake cool in pan on a rack for 30 minutes. Meanwhile, in a small bowl, gently stir together remaining 1 cup sour cream and the 1 tablespoon sugar; cover and refrigerate.

3 Spread cooled cheesecake with sour cream topping. Cover and refrigerate until cold (at least 4 hours) or until next day. Just before serving, sprinkle with cocoa; then remove pan rim. Garnish with chocolate-covered espresso beans.

makes 12 to 16 servings

per serving: 276 calories, 15 g protein, 37 g carbohydrates, 7 g total fat, 62 mg cholesterol, 492 mg sodium

trail mix bars

preparation time: about 1 hour

1 cup all-purpose flour

1 teaspoon baking powder

³/₄ cup *each* golden and dark raisins

¹/₂ cup semisweet chocolate chips

¹/₃ cup butter or margarine,
    at room temperature

¹/₂ cup firmly packed brown sugar

¹/₂ cup smooth unsweetened applesauce

2 large egg whites

2 teaspoons vanilla

1 In a small bowl, stir together flour, baking powder, raisins, and chocolate chips. In a food processor or a large bowl, combine butter, sugar, applesauce, egg whites, and vanilla; whirl or beat with an electric mixer until smoothly blended. Add flour mixture; whirl or beat until dry ingredients are evenly moistened. Spread batter in a lightly greased square 8-inch (nonstick or regular baking pan.

2 Bake in a 325° oven until cookie is golden around edges and a wooden pick inserted in center comes out clean (about 40 minutes; do not pierce chocolate chips). Let cool in pan on a rack. To serve, cut into 2-inch squares.

makes 16 bars

per bar: 163 calories, 2 g protein, 28 g carbohydrates, 6 g total fat, 10 mg cholesterol, 81 mg sodium

cactus pear & tree pear soup

preparation time: about 45 minutes

RED PRICKLY PEAR PURÉE:

About 5 pounds despined red prickly pears (also called cactus pears or tunas)

¹/₃ cup lemon juice

2 tablespoons sugar

RASPBERRY PURÉE:

4 cups fresh or frozen unsweetened raspberries

1 cup orange juice

¹/₃ cup lemon juice

¹/₃ cup sugar

TREE PEAR PURÉE:

2 cans (about 1 lb. *each*) pears in extra-light syrup

1 star anise or 1 teaspoon anise seeds

¹/₄ cup lemon juice

1 tablespoon sugar

GARNISH:

6 to 8 star anise (optional)

Mint sprigs (optional)

1 Prepare red prickly pear purée (Step 2) or raspberry purée (Step 3), then prepare tree pear purée (Step 4).

2 To prepare red prickly pear purée, wear rubber gloves to protect your hands from hidden needles. Cut prickly pears into halves lengthwise. Using a small knife, pull off and discard outer layer (including peel) from fruit; this layer will separate easily. Place fruit in a food processor (a blender will pulverize seeds). Whirl until puréed, then pour into a fine strainer set over a bowl. Firmly rub purée through strainer into bowl; discard seeds. Add lemon juice and sugar. Pour into a small pitcher. (At this point, you may cover and refrigerate until next day; stir before using.)

3 To prepare raspberry purée, in a food processor, whirl raspberries until smoothly puréed (a blender will pulverize seeds). Pour purée into a fine strainer set over a bowl. Firmly rub purée through strainer into bowl; discard seeds. Add orange juice, lemon juice, and sugar. Pour into a small pitcher. (At this point, you may cover and refrigerate until next day; stir before using.)

4 To prepare tree pear purée, drain pears; reserving 1¹/₂ cups of the syrup, discard remainder. In a small pan, combine reserved syrup and 1 star anise or anise seeds. Bring syrup to a boil over high heat; then reduce heat, cover, and simmer very gently until flavors are blended (about 10 minutes). Pour syrup through a fine strainer set over a bowl; discard star anise or seeds. In a food processor or blender, whirl pears until smoothly puréed; then add syrup (if using a blender, add syrup while you are puréeing pears). Stir in lemon juice and sugar. Pour into a small pitcher. (At this point, you may cover and refrigerate until next day; stir before using.)

5 With a pitcher in each hand, simultaneously and gently pour purées into an individual 1¹/₂- to 2-cup soup bowl (wide bowls create the most dramatic effect). Repeat to fill rest of bowls, allowing a total of 1 to 1¹/₂ cups purée for each serving. Garnish each with a star anise and mint sprigs, if desired.

makes 6 to 8 servings

per serving: 187 calories, 2 g protein, 46 g carbohydrates, 1 g total fat, 0 mg cholesterol, 19 mg sodium

sparkling jewels fruit soup

cooking time: about 20 minutes

1 large firm-ripe kiwi fruit, peeled
   and thinly sliced

1/2 cup diced firm-ripe nectarine
   or peeled peach

1/3 cup fresh or frozen unsweetened blueberries

1/3 cup thinly sliced hulled strawberries

1/3 cup very thinly sliced firm-ripe plums

2 tablespoons lemon juice

2 cups white grape juice

2 tablespoons minced crystallized ginger

3 tablespoons orange-flavored liqueur

Mint sprigs (optional)

1 Prepare fruit. Place fruit in a large bowl and mix gently with lemon juice. (At this point, you may cover and refrigerate for up to 2 hours.)

2 In a small pan, bring grape juice and ginger to a boil over high heat. Stir in liqueur; pour over fruit. Ladle soup into bowls; garnish with mint sprigs, if desired.

makes 4 to 6 servings

per serving: 145 calories, 0.5 g protein, 33 g carbohydrates, 0.3 g total fat, 0 mg cholesterol, 15 mg sodium

dessert nachos

preparation time: about 30 minutes

1/3 cup sugar

1 teaspoon ground cinnamon

10 flour tortillas

2 cups strawberries

2 large kiwi fruit

1 cup diced orange segments

1 large package (about 8 oz.) Neufchâtel
   or nonfat cream cheese

1/2 cup orange juice

3 tablespoons honey

1 To prepare nacho chips, in a shallow bowl, combine sugar and cinnamon; set aside. Dip tortillas, one at a time, in water; let drain briefly. Stack tortillas; then cut stack into 6 to 8 wedges. Dip one side of each wedge in sugar mixture. Arrange wedges in a single layer, sugar side up, on lightly oiled 12- by 15-inch baking sheets; do not overlap wedges. Bake in a 500° oven until crisp and golden, 4 to 5 minutes. (At this point, you may cool; then store airtight at room temperature for up to 3 days.)

2 To prepare fruit salsa, hull strawberries; dice into a bowl. Add kiwi fruit and orange segments. Cover and refrigerate until ready to serve or for up to 4 hours.

3 In a small pan, combine Neufchâtel cheese, orange juice, and honey. Whisk over low heat until sauce is smooth (about 3 minutes).

4 Mound chips on a platter. Offer cheese sauce and salsa to spoon onto chips.

makes 10 to 12 servings

per serving: 234 calories, 5 g protein, 37 g carbohydrates, 8 g total fat, 16 mg cholesterol, 236 mg sodium

chocolate banana cobbler

preparation time: about 1 hour

3/4 cup raisins

2 tablespoons light or dark rum

1/2 cup firmly packed brown sugar

1/4 cup half-and-half

2 tablespoons light corn syrup

1/4 teaspoon salt

2 tablespoons lemon juice

1 tablespoon cornstarch

5 large bananas, cut into slanting slices 1/2 inch thick

3/4 cup all-purpose flour

1/2 cup granulated sugar

1/2 cup unsweetened cocoa powder

1/4 teaspoon salt

1/4 teaspoon instant espresso or coffee powder

1/8 teaspoon ground ginger

1/3 cup butter or margarine, cut into chunks

1 In a small bowl, combine raisins and rum. Let stand until raisins are softened (about 10 minutes), stirring occasionally. Meanwhile, in another small bowl, mix brown sugar, half-and-half, corn syrup, and the 1/8 teaspoon salt.

2 In a shallow 1 1/2- to 2-quart casserole, blend lemon juice, cornstarch, and 2 tablespoons water; gently mix in bananas. Add brown sugar mixture and raisin mixture; stir gently to coat fruit. Spread out fruit mixture in an even layer; set aside.

3 In a food processor or a medium-size bowl, whirl or stir together flour, granulated sugar, cocoa, the 1/4 teaspoon salt, instant espresso, and ginger. Add butter; whirl or rub with your fingers until mixture resembles fine crumbs. With your fingers, squeeze mixture to form large lumps; then crumble over banana mixture.

4 Set casserole in a larger baking pan to catch any drips. Bake in a 375° oven until fruit mixture is bubbly in center and topping feels firm when gently pressed (about 35 minutes). Let cool slightly; spoon into bowls.

makes 8 servings

per serving: 385 calories, 4 g protein, 76 g carbohydrates, 10 g total fat, 23 mg cholesterol, 199 mg sodium

---

do-it-yourself chocolate date bars

preparation time: about 15 minutes
chilling time: about 30 minutes

---

1 package (about 6 oz.) semisweet chocolate chips

1 cup chopped pitted dates

1/4 cup light corn syrup

1/2 cup raisins

1 1/2 cups oven-toasted rice cereal

1 In a large microwave-safe bowl, combine chocolate chips, dates, and corn syrup. Microwave on high (100%) for 1 1/2 minutes; stir. Then microwave again on high (100%) for 1 to 1 1/2 more minutes or until chocolate is melted and smooth and dates are soft. Stir in raisins and cereal.

2 Line a flat tray with wax paper. Working quickly, spoon chocolate mixture onto paper into 8 bars, each about 1 inch wide and 5 inches long; smooth with 2 spoons. Refrigerate until firm to the touch (about 30 minutes). If made ahead, wrap bars individually in plastic wrap and refrigerate for up to 2 weeks.

makes 8 bars

per bar: 220 calories, 2 g protein, 46 g carbohydrates, 6 g total fat, 0.2 mg cholesterol, 62 mg sodium

banana streusel bundt cake

preparation time: 20 minutes
cooking time: 60 to 70 minutes
cooling time: 30 minutes

$^1/_2$ **cup all-purpose flour**

$^1/_2$ **cup each sweetened shredded coconut and regular rolled oats**

$^1/_2$ **cup semisweet chocolate chips**

$^1/_4$ **cup firmly packed brown sugar**

1 cup butter or margarine, cut into chunks

1 $^1/_2$ cups coarsely mashed ripe bananas

$^3/_4$ **cup nonfat sour cream**

3 large eggs

2 large egg whites

1 cup granulated sugar

1 $^1/_2$ cups all-purpose flour

1 tablespoon baking powder

1 teaspoon each ground cinnamon and vanilla

$^1/_3$ **cup butter or margarine, melted**

About $^1/_4$ cup powdered sugar

1 In a medium-size bowl, stir together the $^1/_2$ cup flour, coconut, oats, chocolate chips, and brown sugar. Add the $^1/_4$ cup butter and 1 tablespoon water; rub with your fingers until mixture is crumbly and well blended. Set aside.

2 In a food processor or a large bowl, combine bananas, sour cream, eggs, egg whites, and granulated sugar. Whirl or beat with an electric mixer until smooth. Add the 1$^1/_2$ cups flour, baking powder, cinnamon, vanilla, and the $^1/_3$ cup melted butter; whirl or beat until well blended.

3 Sprinkle half the coconut streusel in a well-greased, floured 10-cup nonstick or regular fluted tube pan. Pour half the batter over coconut mixture; then sprinkle with remaining coconut streusel. Pour remaining batter over streusel.

4 Bake in a 350° oven until cake just begins to pull away from side of pan and a wooden pick inserted in center comes out clean (60 to 70 minutes). Let cool in pan on a rack for 30 minutes.

5 Invert pan onto a platter; lift off pan to release cake. If any of the streusel topping sticks to pan bottom, gently remove from pan and arrange atop cake. Sprinkle with powdered sugar.

makes 10 to 12 servings

per serving: 441 calories, 7 g protein, 71 g carbohydrates, 15 g total fat, 84 mg cholesterol, 286 mg sodium

CHEESE WITH FRUIT: For a simple, appealing dessert, serve fresh fruit and a selection of complementary cheeses. Arrange choice whole fruits in a basket, cheeses on a pretty tray; provide cheese cutters and small, sharp knives. Try blue, Gorgonzola, and Roquefort with apples, grapes, and pears; Cheddar with pears and red-skinned apples; Jarlsberg and Gouda with apples, pears, and apricots; Swiss and Emmenthaler with pears; jack or Teleme with apricots, melons, and plums.

pears and cream pie

preparation time: 35 minutes
cooking time: about 1 hour

3/4 cup raisins

3 tablespoons brandy or orange juice

Pie pastry

1 cup nonfat sour cream

1 large egg

1 large egg white

1/2 cup granulated sugar

2 tablespoons all-purpose flour

1 teaspoon vanilla

1/2 teaspoon ground cinnamon

1/4 teaspoon ground nutmeg

1/2 cup firmly packed brown sugar

2/3 cup all-purpose flour

3 tablespoons butter or margarine,
    melted and cooled slightly

2 tablespoons smooth unsweetened applesauce

4 large firm-ripe D'Anjou or Bartlett pears

1. In a large bowl, combine raisins and brandy. Let stand until raisins are softened (about 10 minutes), stirring occasionally.

2. Meanwhile, prepare pie pastry and line pie pan, but do not prick pastry after lining pan. Cover and refrigerate.

3. In a small bowl, combine sour cream, egg, egg white, granulated sugar, the 2 tablespoons flour, vanilla, cinnamon, and nutmeg. Beat until smoothly blended; set aside. In another small bowl, combine brown sugar, the 2/3 cup flour, butter, and applesauce. Stir until mixture is evenly moistened. Then, with your fingers, squeeze mixture to form large lumps; set aside.

4. Peel and core pears; cut into slices about 1/2 inch thick. As pears are sliced, add to bowl with raisin mixture and turn to coat with brandy. Add sour cream mixture to pear mixture; mix gently to coat fruit evenly.

5. Spoon pear filling into pastry shell. Crumble brown sugar mixture evenly over filling.

6. Set pie pan in a larger baking pan to catch any drips. Bake pie on lowest rack of a 375° oven until filling is bubbly in center and topping is browned (about 1 hour); if crust or topping begins to darken excessively, cover it with foil. Let cool on a rack before serving; serve warm.

makes 8 to 10 servings

per serving: 435 calories, 6 g protein, 70 g carbohydrates, 14 g total fat, 34 mg cholesterol, 137 mg sodium

oat, coconut & cocoa drops

preparation time: 20 minutes
standing time: 40 minutes to 1 hour

1/2 cup light corn syrup

1/4 cup granulated sugar

1/4 cup butter or margarine

1/4 cup milk

2 tablespoons unsweetened cocoa powder

2 1/3 cups regular rolled oats

1/2 cup sweetened shredded coconut

About 1/4 cup powdered sugar

1. In a 2-quart glass measuring cup or microwave-safe bowl, combine corn syrup, granulated sugar, butter, and milk. Microwave on high (100%) for 2 minutes; then stir until butter is melted. Microwave on high (100%) again for 30 seconds to 1 minute or until mixture bubbles; then microwave for 30 more seconds. Remove from microwave. Stir in cocoa until well blended; then stir in oats and coconut. Set mixture aside and let cool slightly.

2. To shape candies, roll 1-tablespoon portions of oat mixture into balls. Roll balls in powdered sugar to coat, then place slightly apart on a plate. Let stand or refrigerate until firm (40 minutes to 1 hour). If made ahead, wrap airtight and refrigerate for up to 4 days.

makes 24 candies

per candy: 89 calories, 1 g protein, 15 g carbohydrates, 3 g total fat, 6 mg cholesterol, 333 mg sodium

oatmeal raisin cookies

preparation time: 35 minutes

2 cups all-purpose flour

1 teaspoon *each* baking soda
   and ground cinnamon

¹/₂ teaspoon salt

³/₄ cup butter or margarine,
   at room temperature

1¹/₂ cups firmly packed brown sugar

1 cup nonfat sour cream
   or plain nonfat yogurt

1 teaspoon vanilla

3 cups regular rolled oats

1¹/₂ cups raisins

1 In a medium-size bowl, stir together flour, baking soda, cinnamon, and salt; set aside.

2 In a food processor or a large bowl, combine butter, sugar, sour cream, and vanilla. Whirl or beat with an electric mixer until well blended. Add flour mixture to butter mixture; whirl or beat until dry ingredients are evenly moistened. Stir in oats and raisins.

3 Spoon rounded 1 tablespoon portions of dough onto lightly greased large nonstick or regular baking sheets, spacing cookies about 2 inches apart.

4 Bake in a 350° oven until cookies are firm to the touch (about 15 minutes), switching positions of baking sheets halfway through baking. Let cookies cool on baking sheets for about 3 minutes, then transfer to racks to cool completely.

makes about 4¹/₂ dozen cookies

per cookie: 124 calories, 2 g protein, 21 g carbohydrates, 4 g total fat, 9 mg cholesterol, 97 mg sodium

one-pan s'mores

preparation time: 35 minutes

1¹/₂ cups graham cracker crumbs
   (about twenty square 2-inch crackers)

¹/₄ cup sugar

¹/₄ cup butter or margarine, melted

1 jar (about 7 oz.) marshmallow fluff

²/₃ cup semisweet chocolate chips

¹/₂ cup unsweetened cocoa powder

1¹/₂ cups small marshmallows

1 In a food processor or a medium-size bowl, combine graham cracker crumbs, sugar, butter, and 1 tablespoon water. Whirl or stir with a fork until mixture resembles coarse crumbs. Press crumbs firmly over bottom and about ¹/₂ inch up sides of a lightly greased square 8-inch nonstick or regular baking pan. Bake in a 350° oven until crust feels firm when pressed (about 15 minutes). Let cool completely in pan on a rack.

2 Meanwhile, in a 1¹/₂- to 2-quart pan, combine marshmallow fluff and 1 tablespoon water. Stir constantly over medium-low heat just until fluff is melted and smooth. Remove pan from heat and add chocolate chips; stir constantly until chocolate is melted and mixture is smooth. Add cocoa and stir well. Working quickly, stir in marshmallows just until combined (don't let marshmallows melt). Immediately spoon marshmallow mixture over cooled crust and spread to make level.

3 Cover and refrigerate until firm (at least 1 hour) or for up to 8 hours. To serve, cut into 2-inch squares.

makes 16 bars

per bar: 173 calories, 2 g protein, 30 g carbohydrates, 6 g total fat, 8 mg cholesterol, 105 mg sodium

apricot-amaretto torte

preparation time: 50 minutes

1 tablespoon lemon juice

5 medium-size apricots

1/4 cup slivered almonds

2 large eggs

1 cup sugar

4 to 5 tablespoons almond-flavored liqueur

1/2 teaspoon almond extract

3/4 cup all-purpose flour

2 teaspoons baking powder

1/8 teaspoon salt

1/4 cup butter or margarine, melted and cooled slightly

4 teaspoons cornstarch

1 cup apricot nectar

1/2 cup fresh orange juice

1/2 teaspoon vanilla

1 Pour lemon juice into a medium-size bowl. Quarter and pit apricots; add to bowl and turn to coat with juice. Set aside.

2 In a food processor, whirl almonds until finely ground. (Or finely chop almonds with a knife, then place in a large bowl.) To almonds, add eggs, 1/2 cup of the sugar, 1 tablespoon of the liqueur, and almond extract; whirl or beat with an electric mixer until thick and well blended. Add flour, baking powder, salt, and butter; whirl or beat until well blended. Spread batter in a greased, floured 9-inch cake pan with a removable rim. Decoratively arrange apricots in batter, overlapping as needed; press fruit lightly into batter.

3 Bake in a 375° oven until cake just begins to pull away from side of pan and a wooden pick inserted in center comes out clean (about 25 minutes; pierce cake, not fruit). Let cool slightly on a rack.

4 While cake is cooling, stir together cornstarch and 6 tablespoons of the remaining sugar in a small pan. Whisk in apricot nectar and orange juice; cook over medium-high heat, whisking constantly, until mixture boils and thickens slightly. Remove from heat and stir in vanilla and remaining 3 to 4 tablespoons liqueur; keep warm.

4 Sprinkle cake with remaining 2 tablespoons sugar. Remove pan rim and cut cake into wedges; serve with apricot-orange sauce.

makes 8 servings

per serving: 340 calories, 5 g protein, 54 g carbohydrates, 10 g total fat, 69 mg cholesterol, 240 mg sodium

cantaloupe in raspberry purée

cooking time: about 15 minutes

1 1/2 cups raspberries, rinsed and drained

3 tablespoons sugar

1/4 cup cream sherry

1 medium-size cantaloupe, quartered, seeded, and rind removed

1 In a blender or food processor, whirl raspberries until puréed; press through a fine sieve to remove seeds.

2 In a 1-quart pan, combine raspberry purée, sugar, and sherry. Cook over medium-high heat, stirring, until sugar is dissolved and mixture is boiling. Boil for 30 more seconds. Remove from heat and let cool. (At this point, you may cover and let stand for up to 1 hour.)

3 Thinly slice cantaloupe. Spoon raspberry purée onto individual dessert plates; arrange cantaloupe decoratively over sauce.

makes 4 servings

per serving: 131 calories, 2 g protein, 28 g carbohydrates, 0.6 g total fat, 0 mg cholesterol, 14 mg sodium

angel food cake

preparation time: about 55 minutes

1 cup sifted cake flour

1 1/4 cups granulated sugar

12 egg whites, at room temperature

1/2 teaspoon salt

2 teaspoons cream of tartar

1 1/2 teaspoons vanilla or almond extract

Powdered sugar and sliced fresh strawberries
   (optional)

1 Sift together flour and 1/2 cup of the granulated sugar; sift again and set aside.

2 In large bowl of an electric mixer, beat egg whites on high speed until foamy. Add salt and cream of tartar and continue beating until mixture holds soft peaks. Add remaining sugar, 2 tablespoons at a time, beating well after each addition, until mixture holds stiff, glossy peaks.

3 With a rubber spatula, fold in vanilla. Sprinkle in flour mixture, about 1/4 cup at a time, gently folding in each addition just until blended. Turn batter into an ungreased 10-inch tube pan with a removable bottom; gently smooth top. Slide spatula down outside edge of batter and run around pan to eliminate large air bubbles.

4 Bake in a 375° oven until cake is golden and springs back when lightly pressed (about 35 minutes). Invert pan on a funnel or pop bottle to keep cake from shrinking; let cool completely. Remove from pan and place on a cake plate or platter. Dust with powdered sugar and decorate with strawberries, if desired. Slice with an angel food cake knife or serrated knife.

makes 12 servings

per serving: 128 calories, 4 g protein, 27 g carbohydrates, 0.1 g total fat, 0 mg cholesterol, 146 mg sodium

hot cocoa-mocha fondue

preparation time: 15 minutes

1 cup firmly packed brown sugar

1/2 cup unsweetened cocoa powder

2 tablespoons cornstarch

1 teaspoon instant coffee powder

1/4 cup light corn syrup

1 teaspoon vanilla

2 tablespoons crème de cacao (optional)

Angel food cake cubes, tangerine segments,
   banana slices, pear wedges, whole strawberries,
   and sweet cherries with stems

1 In a 1 1/2-quart pan, combine sugar, cocoa, cornstarch, and instant coffee; stir to blend well. Gradually blend in corn syrup and 1 cup water, stirring until smooth. Then cook over medium-high heat, stirring constantly, until mixture boils and thickens (about 5 minutes).

2 Remove pan from heat and stir in vanilla and, if desired, crème de cacao. Pour fondue into a heatproof serving bowl over a candle warmer or into a small electric slow cooker. Spear cubes of cake and fruits with fondue forks or bamboo skewers and dip into warm fondue; stir fondue occasionally.

makes about 2 cups, 8 servings

per serving: 154 caloriess, 1 g protein, 40 g carbohydrates, 0.7 g total fat, 0 mg cholesterol, 24 mg sodium

pear cobbler with ginger crust

preparation time: 45 to 55 minutes

6 large firm-ripe D'Anjou pears, peeled, cored, and thinly sliced

2 tablespoons lime juice

$^1/_4$ cup pure maple syrup

2 cups finely crushed gingersnaps (about thirty-five 2-inch cookies)

$^2/_3$ cup firmly packed brown sugar

3 tablespoons all-purpose flour

$^1/_4$ cup butter or margarine, melted

1 teaspoon vanilla

1 In a shallow $1^1/_2$- to 2-quart casserole, combine pears and lime juice. Add syrup; mix gently to coat fruit evenly. Spread out fruit in an even layer; set aside.

2 In a food processor or a medium-size bowl, whirl or stir together crushed gingersnaps, sugar, and flour. Add butter and vanilla; whirl or stir until mixture resembles coarse crumbs. With your fingers, squeeze mixture to form large lumps; then crumble evenly over pear mixture.

3 Set casserole in a larger baking pan to catch any drips. Bake in a 325° oven until fruit is tender when pierced and topping feels firm when gently pressed (25 to 35 minutes); if topping begins to darken excessively, cover it with foil. Serve warm; to serve, spoon into bowls.

makes 8 servings

per serving: 370 calories, 3 g protein, 73 g carbohydrates, 9 g total fat, 16 mg cholesterol, 253 mg sodium

apple cobbler with oatmeal chocolate cookie crust

preparation time: 20 minutes
cooking time: about 1 hour

5 tablespoons butter or margarine, at room temperature

1 cup sugar

1 large egg white

1 teaspoon vanilla

$^3/_4$ teaspoon ground cardamom or ground cinnamon

1 cup all-purpose flour

$^3/_4$ cup regular rolled oats

$^1/_2$ cup semisweet chocolate chips

10 large tart apples such as Granny Smith or Gravenstein

$^3/_4$ cup sugar

1 tablespoon cornstarch

$1^1/_2$ teaspoons ground cinnamon

$^1/_2$ teaspoon ground allspice

1 In a food processor or a large bowl, combine butter and the 1 cup sugar; whirl or beat with an electric mixer until smooth. Add egg white, vanilla, and cardamom; whirl or beat until blended. Stir in flour, oats, and chocolate chips; set aside. (At this point, you may wrap crust mixture airtight and refrigerate until next day.)

2 peel, core, and slice apples; arrange in a shallow 3- to $3^1/_2$-quart casserole. Sprinkle with the $^3/_4$ cup sugar, cornstarch, cinnamon, and allspice; mix gently to coat fruit with sugar mixture, then spread out fruit mixture in an even layer. Crumble oat mixture over fruit mixture.

3 Set casserole in a larger baking pan to catch any drips. Bake in a 350° oven until fruit mixture is bubbly in center and topping is richly browned (about 1 hour). Serve warm or at room temperature; to serve, spoon into bowls.

makes 8 servings

per serving: 516 calories, 4 g protein, 105 g carbohydrates, 11 g total fat, 19 mg cholesterol, 82 mg sodium

chocolate cherry brownies

preparation time: 20 minutes
cooking time: 45 to 50 minutes

1 package (about 5 oz.) pitted dried cherries, chopped

4 cup kirsch or berry liqueur

1/2 cup butter or margarine, cut into chunks

4 ounces unsweetened chocolate, coarsely chopped

2 cups sugar

2 teaspoons vanilla

1/4 to 1/2 teaspoon instant espresso or coffee powder

2 large egg whites

2 large eggs

1 cup all-purpose flour

1/2 teaspoon each baking powder and salt

3/4 to 1 cup cherry preserves

1 In a small bowl, combine dried cherries and liqueur; let stand until cherries are softened (about 15 minutes), stirring occasionally.

2 Meanwhile, melt butter in a 4- to 5-quart pan over medium-low heat. Remove pan from heat, add chocolate, and stir until chocolate is melted and mixture is smooth. Let cool for 10 minutes. Add sugar, vanilla, and instant espresso. Mix well. Beat in egg whites; then add whole eggs, one at a time, beating well after each addition. Add dried cherry mixture, flow baking powder, and salt; stir until all ingredients are evenly moistened.

3 Spoon two-thirds of the batter into lightly greased and floured 9- by 13-inch baking pan; spread to make level. Drop preserves by spoonfuls over batter and gently spread out evenly. Drop remaining batter by spoonfuls over preserves; swirl with a knife to blend batter slightly with preserves.

4 Bake in a 350° oven until a wooden pick inserted in center comes out clean (45 to 50 minutes). Let cool in pan on a rack, then cut into about 2-inch squares.

makes 24 brownies

per brownie: 200 calories, 2 g protein, 35 g carbohydrates, 7 g total fat, 28 mg cholesterol, 110 mg sodium

creamy gingered cheese dip

preparation time: 5 minutes

1 1/2 cups low-fat (2%) cottage cheese

1/4 cup powdered sugar

1 tablespoon lemon juice

1 teaspoon vanilla

2 tablespoons chopped preserved ginger in syrup

2 tablespoons nonfat milk

Large whole strawberries, preferably with stems

1 In a food processor or blender, combine cottage cheese, sugar, lemon juice, vanilla, ginger, and milk. Whirl until smooth; scrape down side of container occasionally.

2 Transfer dip to a serving bowl. If made ahead, cover and refrigerate until next day. To serve, place bowl of dip on a tray and surround with strawberries for dipping.

makes about 1 3/4 cups, 6 to 8 servings

per serving: 80 calories, 7 g protein, 11 g carbohydrates, 0.9 g total fat, 4 mg cholesterol, 202 mg sodium

drunken cake

preparation time: about 30 minutes

1 1/4 cups sugar

2 tablespoons plus 1 teaspoon grated orange peel

1/2 cup orange juice

1/2 teaspoon grated lemon peel

2 tablespoons lemon juice

1/8 teaspoon ground cinnamon

2 to 3 tablespoons light or dark rum

1 teaspoon vanilla

2 large eggs

3/4 cup all-purpose flour

1 1/2 teaspoons baking powder

1/4 cup butter or margarine, melted

Mint sprigs

1 To prepare syrup, in a small pan, mix 3/4 cup of the sugar, 1 teaspoon of the orange peel, orange juice, lemon peel, lemon juice, and cinnamon. Bring to a boil over medium-high heat. Boil, stirring, just until sugar is dissolved. Remove pan from heat and let cool; then stir in rum and vanilla; set aside.

2 In a food processor, whirl eggs and remaining 1/2 cup sugar until thick and lemon-colored. Add flour, baking powder, butter, and remaining 2 tablespoons orange peel to processor; whirl until well blended. Spread batter in a greased, floured 9-inch cake pan with a removable rim. Bake in a 375° oven until cake just begins to pull away from sides of pan and center springs back when lightly pressed with a finger (about 20 minutes).

3 Set warm cake in pan on a rack; set rack over a plate to catch any drips of syrup. Pierce cake all over with a fork. Slowly pour syrup over cake; let cake cool. Just before serving, remove pan rim. Garnish cake with mint sprigs.

makes 8 servings

per serving: 259 calories, 3 g protein, 43 g carbohydrates, 8 g total fat, 69 mg cholesterol, 167 mg sodium

honeydew melon dessert bowl

preparation time: about 30 minutes

FRUIT:

2 medium-size honeydew melons

1 large can (about 20 oz.) or 2 cans (about 11 oz. *each*) litchis

10 to 16 strawberries, hulled and halved

STRAWBERRY SAUCE:

3 cups strawberries, hulled

2 tablespoons lemon juice

1 tablespoon sugar, or to taste

1 Cut off top third of each melon. Scoop out seeds; scoop fruit into balls or chunks from shells and from top slices, removing as much melon as possible. Discard top slices.

2 Place melon pieces in a bowl. Drain litchis, reserving 1/2 cup of the syrup for the Strawberry Sauce (discard remaining syrup). Add litchis and halved strawberries to melon pieces; mix gently. Spoon fruit into melon shells.

3 To prepare strawberry sauce, in a blender or food processor, combine hulled whole strawberries, the 1/2 cup reserved litchi syrup, lemon juice, and sugar. Whirl until smooth. (At this point, you may cover and refrigerate fruit salad and sauce separately for up to 4 hours.)

4 Serve fruit in melons with strawberry sauce.

makes 8 to 10 servings

per serving: 116 calories, 1 g protein, 30 g carbohydrates, 0.5 g total fat, 0 mg cholesterol, 37 mg sodium

cinnamon bread pudding with pumpkin custard

preparation time: 50 minutes

$3/4$ cup raisins

8 to 10 ounces unsliced day-old crusty sourdough bread

$1/4$ cup butter or margarine, melted

$3/4$ cup sugar

2 teaspoons ground cinnamon

3 large eggs

2 $3/4$ cups low-fat (2%) milk

1 can (about 1 lb.) pumpkin

$1/2$ teaspoon ground nutmeg

1 teaspoon vanilla

1 In a small bowl, combine raisins and $3/4$ cup hot water; let stand until raisins are softened (about 10 minutes), stirring occasionally.

2 Meanwhile, tear bread into about 1-inch chunks; you should have about 6 cups. Place bread in a large bowl and mix in butter. In a small bowl, combine $1/4$ cup of the sugar with cinnamon; sprinkle over bread, then mix gently but thoroughly. In another small bowl, beat one of the eggs with $3/4$ cup of the milk until blended; gently mix into bread mixture. Drain raisins well; add to bread mixture and mix just until evenly distributed.

3 Spoon bread mixture into a greased shallow $1^{1}/2$- to 2-quart baking dish. Bake in a 375° oven until crisp and deep brown (about 30 minutes).

4 Meanwhile, in the top of a 2- to 3-quart double boiler, combine remaining $1/2$ cup sugar, remaining 2 eggs, remaining 2 cups milk, pumpkin, nutmeg, and vanilla. Beat until blended. Then set over simmering water and cook, stirring often, until custard is steaming and thickly coats a metal spoon (about 12 minutes). Keep warm.

5 To serve, pour custard into individual bowls; spoon warm bread pudding on top.

makes 6 servings

per serving: 466 calories, 12 g protein, 74 g carbohydrates, 15 g total fat, 136 mg cholesterol, 431 mg sodium

peppermint fudge

preparation time: 20 minutes
chilling time: at least 2 hours

$1/2$ cup evaporated skim milk

1 $1/4$ cups sugar

$1/4$ teaspoon salt

$1/4$ cup butter or margarine

1 package (about 6 oz.) semisweet chocolate chips

$3/4$ cup marshmallow fluff

1 teaspoon vanilla

$1/2$ cup crushed hard peppermint candy

1 In a heavy $2^{1}/2$- to 3-quart pan, combine milk, sugar, salt, and butter. Bring to a rolling boil over medium-low heat, stirring; then boil for 5 minutes, stirring constantly and reducing heat as needed to prevent scorching.

2 Remove pan from heat; add chocolate chips and stir until melted. Quickly stir in marshmallow fluff and vanilla; then mix in peppermint candy until blended. Pour into a buttered square 8-inch baking pan; spread to make an even layer. Let cool, then cover and refrigerate until firm (at least 2 hours). To serve, cut into 1-inch squares. If made ahead, wrap airtight and refrigerate for up to 2 weeks.

makes 64 pieces

per piece: 45 calories, 0.3 g protein, 2 g total fat, 8 g carbohydrates, 2 mg cholesterol, 21 mg sodium

minted poached pears

preparation time: about 40 minutes

2 cans (12 oz. *each***) unsweetened pineapple juice**

**4 medium-size firm-ripe Bosc, d'Anjou,
    or Comice pears**

**2 tablespoons crème de menthe
    or** **¹/₄ teaspoon mint extract**

Mint sprigs

1 Pour juice into a 3-quart pan and place over medium heat. Peel pears, leaving some peel around stems; do not remove stems. With an apple corer, cut out blossom end and core from each pear. Place pears in juice and bring to a boil; reduce heat, cover, and simmer until pears are tender when pierced (about 20 minutes).

2 With a slotted spoon, lift out pears and place in a serving dish. Increase heat to high and boil juice, uncovered, stirring often, until reduced to about 1 cup (about 10 minutes). Stir in crème de menthe. Pour over pears. Serve warm; or cool, cover, and refrigerate until chilled and serve cold. Garnish with mint sprigs.

makes 4 servings

per serving: 229 calories, 1 g protein, 53 g carbohydrates, 0.8 g total fat, 0 mg cholesterol, 2 mg sodium

cranberry-walnut bars

preparation time: 20 minutes
cooking time: about 1 hour

1 cup dried cranberries

**3 tablespoons orange-flavored liqueur or orange
    juice**

1 ¹/₄ cups all-purpose flour

¹/₄ cup powdered sugar

¹/₈ teaspoon salt

¹/₃ cup butter or margarine, cut into chunks

**1 tablespoon apple jelly, melted and cooled
    slightly**

1 large egg

2 large egg whites

²/₃ cup light corn syrup

²/₃ cup granulated sugar

1 teaspoon vanilla

1 cup fresh or frozen cranberries, chopped

¹/₂ cup chopped walnuts

1 In a small bowl, combine dried cranberries and liqueur; let stand until cranberries are softened (about 10 minutes), stirring occasionally.

2 In a food processor or a medium-size bowl, whirl or stir together flour, powdered sugar, and salt. Add butter and jelly; whirl or rub with your fingers until mixture resembles coarse crumbs. Press crumbs firmly over bottom and about 16 inch up sides of a lightly greased square 8-inch nonstick or regular baking pan. Prick dough all over with a fork. Bake in a 350° oven until pale golden (about 15 minutes).

3 Meanwhile, in a large bowl, beat whole egg, egg whites, corn syrup, granulated sugar, and vanilla until smoothly blended. Stir in fresh cranberries, dried cranberry-liqueur mixture, and walnuts. Remove hot baked crust from oven; pour filling into crust. Return to oven and bake until filling no longer jiggles in center when pan is gently shaken (35 to 40 minutes; cover edge of crust with foil if it begins to brown excessively). Let cool in pan on a rack. Serve at room temperature or chilled; to serve, cut into 2-inch squares.

makes 16 bars

per bar: 218 calories, 2 g protein, 37 g carbohydrates, 7 g total fat, 24 mg cholesterol, 84 mg sodium

peach shortcakes

preparation time: about 35 minutes

1 cup all-purpose flour

2 teaspoons baking powder

1/4 teaspoon baking soda

3 tablespoons margarine

1/3 cup low-fat buttermilk

1 cup low-fat cottage cheese

About 3 tablespoons honey

1/8 teaspoon ground nutmeg

2 large firm-ripe peaches

1 In a medium-size bowl, stir together flour, baking powder, and baking soda until well blended. Using a pastry blender or your fingers, cut in or rub in margarine until mixture resembles coarse meal. Add buttermilk and stir just until dry ingredients are evenly moistened.

2 Turn dough out onto a lightly floured board and knead gently just until smooth (about 1 minute). Divide dough into fourths. Pat each portion into a 3-inch-diameter round; place rounds well apart on an increased baking sheet.

3 Bake in a 450° oven until lightly browned (about 15 minutes). Transfer to a rack and let cool slightly.

4 Meanwhile, whirl cottage cheese, 3 tablespoons of the honey, and nutmeg in a blender or food processor until smooth. Peel, then pit and slice peaches.

5 To serve, split each biscuit in half horizontally. Set bottom halves on 4 plates; top each with a fourth of the cottage cheese mixture and a fourth of the peach slices. Cover lightly with biscuit tops. Serve with additional honey, if desired.

makes 4 servings

per serving: 345 calories, 13 g protein, 52 g carbohydrates, 10 g total fat, 6 mg cholesterol, 663 mg sodium

hot cranberry fondue

preparation time: 25 minutes

1 cup dried cranberries

1 cup ruby port

2/3 cup sugar

1 cinnamon stick (about 3 inches long)

1 tablespoon grated orange peel

2 tablespoons orange flavored liqueur (optional)

1 In a 1 1/2- to 2-quart pan, combine cranberries, port, 1/2 cup water, sugar, cinnamon stick, and orange peel. Bring to a boil over medium-high heat, stirring until sugar is dissolved. Then continue to cook until mixture is reduced to about 1 1/2 cups, about 15 minutes; stir occasionally at first, more often as mixture thickens toward end of cooking time.

2 Remove from heat and stir in liqueur, if desired. Remove and discard cinnamon stick. Transfer mixture to a blender or food processor and whirl until coarsely pureed. Pour fondue into a heatproof serving bowl over a candle warmer or into a small electric slow cooker. Pick up apple wedges with your fingers (or spear them with fondue forks or bamboo skewers) and dip into warm fondue.

makes about 1 1/2 cups, 6 servings

per serving: 209 calories, 0.01 g protein, 42 g carbohydrates, 0.3 g total fat, 0 mg cholesterol, 4 mg sodium

chocolate biscotti

preparation time: about 1 hour

**¹/₄ cup butter or margarine,
    at room temperature**

¹/₈ cup granulated sugar

4 large egg whites

2 cups all-purpose flour

¹/₃ cup unsweetened cocoa powder

2 teaspoons baking powder

¹/₃ cup sifted powdered sugar

About 2 teaspoons low-fat (1%) milk

1 In a large bowl, beat butter and granulated sugar until fluffy. Add egg whites and beat until well blended. In a medium bowl, combine flour, cocoa, and baking powder; add to butter mixture and stir until well blended.

2 Turn dough out onto a large nonstick or lightly greased regular baking sheet. Shape dough down length of sheet into a loaf about 2¹/₂ inches wide and ⁵/₈ inch thick. Bake in a 350° oven until crusty and firm to the touch (about 20 minutes).

3 Remove baking sheet from oven and let loaf cool for 3 to 5 minutes; then cut diagonally into slices about ¹/₂ inch thick. Tip slices cut side down on baking sheet. Return to oven and bake until biscotti feel firm and dry (15 to 20 minutes). Transfer to racks and let cool.

4 In a small bowl, stir together powdered sugar and 2 teaspoons of the milk, or enough to make a pourable icing. Using a spoon, drizzle icing decoratively over biscotti. Let stand until icing is firm before serving.

makes about 1 ¹/₂ dozen cookies

per cookie: 112 calories, 3 g protein, 19 g carbohydrates, 3 g total fat, 7 mg cholesterol, 97 mg sodium

cherry-blueberry crisp

preparation time: about 1¹/₄ hours

¹/₃ cup firmly packed brown sugar

2 tablespoons all-purpose flour

¹/₂ teaspoon ground cinnamon

**3 cups pitted fresh Bing
    or other dark sweet cherries**

2 cups fresh blueberries

1 tablespoon lemon juice

1 cup quick-cooking rolled oats

¹/₄ cup firmly packed brown sugar

**¹/₄ teaspoon *each* ground cinnamon
    and ground ginger**

3 tablespoons butter or margarine, melted

1 In a shallow 2-quart casserole, stir together the ¹/₃ cup sugar, flour, and cinnamon. Add cherries, blueberries, and lemon juice; mix gently to coat fruit with sugar mixture. Spread out fruit mixture in an even layer.

2 In a small bowl, combine oats, the ¹/₄ cup sugar, cinnamon, and ginger; add butter and stir with a fork until mixture is crumbly. Sprinkle mixture evenly over fruit.

3 Set casserole in a larger baking pan to catch any drips. Bake in a 350° oven until fruit mixture is bubbly in center and topping is golden brown (35 to 40 minutes); if topping begins to darken excessively, cover it with foil. Serve hot, warm, or at room temperature. To serve, spoon into bowls.

makes 6 servings

per serving: 273 calories, 4 g protein, 51 g carbohydrates, 7 g total fat, 16 mg cholesterol, 71 mg sodium

tropical sherbet

preparation time: 1 hour
cooking time: about 10 minutes
chilling time: about 2 hours (for Frozen Citrus Bowls)
freezing time: about 2 ½ hours for Frozen Citrus Bowls, about 3 hours for sherbert

Frozen Citrus Bowls (recipe follows)

5 or 6 medium-size firm-ripe mangoes

6 tablespoons lime juice

1 can (about 14 oz.) mango nectar

1 jar (about 7 oz.) marshmallow fluff

2 medium-size ripe bananas

¹/₂ cup low-fat (2%) milk

Mint sprigs (optional)

1 Prepare Frozen Citrus Bowls; keep frozen.

2 Peel 1 mango; thinly slice fruit from pit into a food processor or blender. Add 2 tablespoons of the lime juice. Then add half *each* of the mango nectar, marshmallow fluff, bananas, and milk. Whirl until smooth, scraping sides of container often; transfer to a bowl. Smoothly purée remaining mango nectar, marshmallow fluff, bananas, and milk; pour into bowl.

3 Pour fruit mixture into a metal pan, 8 or 9 inches square. Cover and freeze until solid (about 3 hours) or for up to 1 week. Break into small chunks with a heavy spoon; whirl in a food processor or beat with an electric mixer until smooth. Serve; or, for firmer sherbet, freeze for up to 1 more hour. If made ahead, pack into containers, cover, and freeze for up to 1 week; before serving, whirl or beat until soft enough to scoop.

4 Just before serving, peel remaining 4 or 5 mangoes; thinly slice fruit from pits into a large bowl. Add remaining ¹/₄ cup lime juice; mix gently to coat.

5 Serve sherbet in Frozen Citrus Bowls; garnish with mint sprigs, if desired. Drain mangoes and serve alongside.

makes 6 servings

per serving: 392 calories, 4 g protein, 108 g carbohydrates, 1 g total fat, 2 mg cholesterol, 39 mg sodium

FROZEN CITRUS BOWLS

1 In a 1- to 2-quart pan, combine ¹/₂ cup sugar and ¹/₂ cup water. Bring to a boil over high heat, stirring occasionally. Remove from heat and let cool; then refrigerate until very cold (about 2 hours).

2 Meanwhile, with a sharp knife, cut 2 *each* lemons, limes, and oranges (or use all one kind of fruit) into even, paper-thin slices, ¹/₁₆ to ¹/₈ inch thick. Line six 1¹/₂- to 2-cup bowls (2 to 2¹/₂ inches deep) with plastic wrap. Selecting the prettiest citrus slices, dip them in cold sugar syrup; lift out slices and drain briefly, then use to line bottoms and sides of bowls snugly, overlapping as needed. Reserve any leftover syrup and citrus slices for other uses.

3 Wrap bowls airtight and freeze until fruit is firm (about 2¹/₂ hours) or for up to 1 week. To use, gently lift frozen citrus bowls from molds. Working quickly, peel off plastic wrap, place each bowl on a dessert plate, and fill with sherbet. Serve filled bowls immediately (they keep their shape for only about 15 minutes); or return to freezer for up to 1 hour, then serve.

makes 6 bowls

chocolate hazelnut cake

preparation time: 40 minutes
chilling time: at least 2 hours

2 tablespoons hazelnuts

1 purchased nonfat chocolate loaf cake
(about 15 oz.)

1/2 cup purchased hazelnut-cocoa spread

1 small package (about 6 oz.) semisweet
chocolate chips

2 cups sifted powdered sugar

1 large package (about 8 oz.)
Neufchâtel cheese, cut into chunks

1/2 cup unsweetened cocoa powder

4 cups nonfat sour cream

2 teaspoons vanilla

1 Toast and coarsely chop hazelnuts as directed for Pear &
Hazelnut Upside-down Cake (page 579). Set aside.

2 Cut cake in half horizontally. Set bottom half, cut side up, on a
serving plate. Stir hazelnut-cocoa spread to soften, if necessary;
then spread evenly over cake to within about 1/2 inch of edges.
Place top half of cake, cut side down, over filling; press lightly.

3 Place chocolate chips in a metal bowl nested over a pan of hot
(not boiling) water. Stir often until chocolate is melted and
smooth. Remove from heat and transfer to a food processor or
blender; let stand for 2 to 3 minutes to cool slightly. Add powdered sugar, Neufchâtel cheese, cocoa, sour cream, and vanilla;
whirl until smooth, scraping sides of container often. Let frosting cool slightly; it should be spreadable, but not too soft.

4 Generously spread frosting over sides and top of cake. Cover
cake with a cake cover or an inverted bowl (don't let cover
touch frosting); refrigerate until cold (at least 2 hours) or until
next day. Sprinkle with hazelnuts, pressing them lightly into
frosting. Cut into slices to serve.

makes 10 servings

per serving: 401 calories, 7 g protein, 67 g carbohydrates, 13 g total fat, 11 mg cholesterol,
324 mg sodium

raisin snack cake

preparation time: 20 minutes
cooking time: about 55 minutes

3 cups all-purpose flour

2 cups granulated sugar

2 teaspoons baking soda

1 1/2 teaspoons ground cinnamon

1/2 teaspoon *each* ground nutmeg and salt

1/4 teaspoon ground cloves

1 cup reduced-fat mayonnaise

1/3 cup nonfat milk

2 large eggs

3 large Golden Delicious apples

1 cup *each* golden and dark raisins

1/4 cup powdered sugar

1 In a large bowl, stir together flour, granulated sugar, baking
soda, cinnamon, nutmeg, salt, and cloves; set aside.

2 In a food processor or another large bowl, combine mayonnaise, milk, and eggs; whirl or beat with an electric mixer until
smooth. Set aside. Peel, core, and coarsely chop apples; stir
apples into egg mixture. Then add flour mixture to egg mixture
and whirl or beat just until dry ingredients are evenly moistened. Stir in raisins.

3 Spoon batter into a lightly greased 9- by 13-inch nonstick or regular baking pan; smooth top. Bake in a 350° oven until a wooden
pick inserted in center comes out clean (about 55 minutes).

4 Let cake cool completely in pan on a rack. Just before serving,
sprinkle with powdered sugar. To serve, cut into about 2-inch
squares.

makes 24 servings

per serving: 213 calories, 3 g protein 45 g carbohydrates, 3 g total fat, 18 mg cholesterol,
241 mg sodium

zabaglione cream over warm fruit compote

preparation time: 15 minutes
cooking time: about 40 minutes

1 package (about 12 oz.) mixed dried fruit (whole or halved fruits, not dried fruit bits)

1 1/2 cups white grape juice

1/4 to 1/2 teaspoon ground cinnamon

3 whole cloves

6 large egg yolks

3 tablespoons sugar

1/2 cup Marsala

2 cups frozen reduced-calorie whipped topping, thawed

1 Cut large pieces of fruit into bite-size chunks; set fruit aside. In a medium-size pan, combine grape juice, cinnamon, and cloves; bring to a boil over high heat. Stir in fruit; then reduce heat, cover, and simmer until fruit is plump and tender when pierced (about 30 minutes). Remove from heat and keep warm.

2 In the top of a double boiler, combine egg yolks and sugar. Beat with an electric mixer on high speed or with a whisk until thick and lemon-colored. Beat in Marsala. Set double boiler over (not in) gently simmering water; beat mixture constantly just until it is thick enough to retain a slight peak briefly when beater or whisk is withdrawn (3 to 6 minutes).

3 Working quickly, pour warm egg mixture into a large bowl. Fold in about a third of the whipped topping to lighten egg mixture; then fold in remaining whipped topping. Serve immediately.

4 To serve, lift fruit from pan with a slotted spoon and divide among six 8-ounce stemmed glasses; discard cooking liquid or reserve for other uses. Top with zabaglione cream.

makes 6 servings

per serving: 346 calories, 4 g protein, 61 g carbohydrates, 8 g total fat, 213 mg cholesterol, 24 mg sodium

amaretti-topped raspberry-peach bake

preparation time: about 1 hour

1 tablespoon cornstarch

1/2 teaspoon ground nutmeg

1/3 cup sugar

4 cups peeled, sliced peaches

1 cup fresh raspberries

1 1/2 cups coarsely crushed crisp almond macaroons (about thirty 1 3/4-inch cookies)

1 In a shallow 1 1/2- to 2-quart casserole, stir together cornstarch, nutmeg, and sugar. Add peaches and raspberries; mix gently to coat fruit with sugar mixture. Spread out fruit mixture in an even layer; then sprinkle evenly with crushed macaroons.

2 Bake in a 375° oven until fruit mixture is bubbly in center (40 to 45 minutes); cover with foil during last 10 to 12 minutes of baking if topping begins to darken excessively. Serve warm or at room temperature; to serve, spoon into bowls.

makes 6 servings

per serving: 159 calories, 3 g protein, 32 g carbohydrates, 3 g total fat, 0 mg cholesterol, 9 mg sodium

chocolate shortbread

preparation time: about 40 minutes

**1 cup chocolate graham cracker crumbs
(about twelve 2-inch square crackers)**

$^3/_4$ cup all-purpose flour

$^2/_3$ cup plus $^1/_2$ cup powdered sugar

**$^1/_2$ cup plus 1 tablespoon unsweetened
cocoa powder**

$^1/_2$ teaspoon instant espresso or coffee powder

$^1/_4$ teaspoon salt

$^1/_4$ cup butter or margarine, cut into chunks

$^1/_4$ teaspoon vanilla

About 1 tablespoon nonfat milk

1 In a food processor or a large bowl, whirl or stir together graham cracker crumbs and 1 tablespoon water until crumbs are evenly moistened. Press crumbs evenly over bottom of a lightly greased 9-inch nonstick or regular cheesecake pan with a removable rim; set aside.

2 In food processor or bowl, whirl or stir together flour, the $^2/_3$ cup powdered sugar, the $^1/_2$ cup cocoa, 2 teaspoons water, instant espresso, and salt. Add butter; whirl or rub with your fingers until mixture resembles coarse crumbs.

3 Evenly distribute crumbly dough over graham cracker crumbs in pan. With fingers, press out dough firmly to make an even layer that adheres to graham cracker crumbs (if dough is sticky, lightly flour your fingers).

4 Bake in a 325° oven until shortbread smells toasted and feels firm in center when gently pressed (about 25 minutes). Let shortbread cool in pan on a rack for 5 minutes. Then, using a very sharp knife, cut shortbread, still in pan, into 12 equal wedges. Let cool completely in pan on rack.

5 Meanwhile, in a small bowl, stir together remaining $^1/_2$ cup powdered sugar, remaining 1 tablespoon cocoa, vanilla, and 1 tablespoon of the milk. Beat until smooth; if necessary, add more milk to make glaze easy to drizzle. Remove pan rim from shortbread; drizzle glaze over shortbread. Let stand until glaze is set.

makes 12 servings

per serving: 148 calories, 2 g protein, 25 g carbohydrates, 5 g total fat, 10 mg cholesterol, 137 mg sodium

chocolate taffies

preparation time: 20 to 25 minutes

1 can (about 14 oz.) sweetened condensed milk

1 cup unsweetened cocoa powder

About 1 tablespoon butter or margarine

3 $^1/_2$ ounces chocolate sprinkles (about $^1/_2$ cup)

1 In a 2- to 3-quart pan, combine milk, cocoa, and butter. Place over medium-low heat; cook, stirring, until mixture begins to bubble. Then continue to stir until mixture holds together as a soft mass when pushed to side of pan (3 to 5 minutes). Remove from heat and let stand until cool enough to touch.

2 Spread chocolate sprinkles on a plate. With lightly buttered hands, shape cocoa mixture into 1-inch balls. Roll balls, 4 or 5 at a time, in sprinkles to coat. If desired, place each candy in a small paper or foil bonbon cup. Serve at room temperature. If made ahead, cover airtight and refrigerate for up to 1 week; freeze for longer storage.

makes about 34 candies

per candy: 59 calories, 1 g protein, 11 g carbohydrates, 2 g total fat, 5 mg cholesterol, 21 mg sodium

jumbleberry crumble

preparation time: 15 minutes, plus 15 minutes for filling to stand
cooking time: 50 to 60 minutes

2/3 cup granulated sugar

3 tablespoons quick-cooking tapioca

1 1/2 cups fresh blueberries

1 1/2 cups fresh raspberries

3 cups hulled, halved strawberries

1/2 cup quick-cooking rolled oats

1/2 cup firmly packed brown sugar

1/2 cup all-purpose flour

1 teaspoon ground cinnamon

1/3 cup butter or margarine, melted

1 In a shallow 2-quart casserole, stir together granulated sugar and tapioca. Add blueberries, raspberries, and strawberries; mix gently to coat fruit with sugar mixture. Let stand for 15 minutes to soften tapioca, stirring occasionally; then spread out fruit mixture in an even layer.

2 In a small bowl, combine oats, brown sugar, flour, and cinnamon. Add butter and stir with a fork until mixture is crumbly. Sprinkle topping evenly over fruit mixture.

3 Set casserole in a larger baking pan to catch any drips. Bake in a 350° oven until fruit mixture is bubbly in center and topping is crisp and brown (50 to 60 minutes); if topping begins to darken excessively, cover it with foil. Serve hot, warm, or at room temperature; to serve, spoon into bowls.

makes 6 to 8 servings

per serving: 330 calories, 3 g protein, 61 g carbohydrates, 10 g total fat, 23 mg cholesterol, 117 mg sodium

panforte

preparation time: 25 minutes
cooking time: about 1 1/4 hours

1 cup salted roasted almonds, coarsely chopped

1 cup dried pitted tart cherries

1 cup *each* candied orange peel and candied lemon peel, finely chopped

1 teaspoon each grated lemon peel and ground cinnamon

1/2 teaspoon ground coriander

1/4 teaspoon each ground cloves and ground nutmeg

1/2 cup all-purpose flour

3/4 cup granulated sugar

3/4 cup honey

2 tablespoons butter or margarine

1/2 cup sifted powdered sugar

1 In a large bowl, combine almonds, cherries, candied orange peel, candied lemon peel, grated lemon peel, cinnamon, coriander, cloves, nutmeg, and flour. Mix until nuts and fruit pieces are thoroughly coated with flour; set aside.

2 In a deep medium-size pan, combine granulated sugar, honey, and butter. Cook over high heat, stirring often, until mixture registers 265° (hard-ball stage) on a candy thermometer. Working quickly, pour hot syrup over fruit mixture and mix thoroughly. Immediately scrape mixture into a heavily greased, floured 8- to 9-inch cake pan.

3 Bake in a 300° oven for 1 hour; if cake begins to brown excessively, drape it loosely with foil (don't let foil touch cake). Let cool completely in pan on a rack.

4 Sprinkle a work surface with half the powdered sugar. Using a slender knife and spatula, loosen sides and bottom of cake from pan, then invert cake (prying gently, if needed) onto sugared surface. Sprinkle and pat sugar over entire cake. Then dust cake with remaining powdered sugar to coat completely. Transfer to a platter. To serve, cut into wedges.

makes 12 servings

per serving: 370 calories, 4 g protein, 71 g carbohydrates, 10 g total fat, 5 mg cholesterol, 131 mg sodium

pear & hazelnut upside-down cake

preparation time: 35 minutes
cooking time: about 55 minutes
cooling time: 30 minutes

$^1/_4$ cup hazelnuts

$^1/_2$ cup butter or margarine, melted

$^1/_3$ cup firmly packed brown sugar

2 medium-size firm-ripe pears

1 tablespoon lemon juice

$^1/_4$ cup all-purpose flour

3 large eggs

2 large egg whites

$^1/_2$ cup smooth unsweetened applesauce

2 tablespoons hazelnut-flavored liqueur

1 cup granulated sugar

1 $^1/_2$ cups all-purpose flour

1 tablespoon baking powder

1 teaspoon ground cinnamon

$^1/_2$ teaspoon ground ginger

$^1/_2$ cup firmly packed brown sugar

$^1/_4$ cup half-and-half

2 tablespoons light corn syrup

1 tablespoon butter or margarine

1 tablespoon cornstarch blended
   with 2 tablespoons cold water

$^1/_2$ teaspoon grated lemon peel

$^1/_8$ teaspoon salt

1 $^1/_2$ teaspoons lemon juice

1 Spread hazelnuts in a single layer in a shallow baking pan. Bake in a 375° oven until nuts are golden beneath skins (about 10 minutes). Let nuts cool slightly; then pour into a towel, fold to enclose, and rub to remove as much of loose skins as possible. Let cool; then coarsely chop and set aside.

2 Pour half the melted butter into a well-greased, floured 3- to 3 $^1/_2$-quart nonstick or regular fluted tube pan. Sprinkle with the $^1/_3$ cup brown sugar; set aside. Core pears and cut into $^1/_2$-inch slices. Dip slices into the 1 tablespoon lemon juice; then coat slices with the $^1/_4$ cup flour and arrange decoratively in pan over sugar mixture (overlap slices, if necessary). Set pan aside.

3 In a food processor or a large bowl, combine eggs, egg whites, applesauce, liqueur, and granulated sugar. Whirl or beat with an electric mixer until mixture is thick and lemon-colored. Add the 1 $^1/_2$ cups flour, baking powder, cinnamon, ginger, and remaining melted butter; whirl or beat until dry ingredients are evenly moistened. Carefully pour batter over pears.

4 Bake in a 375° oven until cake just begins to pull away from side of pan and a wooden pick inserted in center of cake comes out clean (about 40 minutes). Let cake cool in pan on a rack for 30 minutes.

5 Meanwhile, in a 1- to 1 $^1/_2$-quart pan, combine the $^1/_2$ cup brown sugar, half-and-half, corn syrup, the 1 tablespoon butter, cornstarch mixture, lemon peel, and salt. Bring to a boil over medium heat. Boil gently, stirring, until slightly thickened (4 to 5 minutes). Remove pan from heat and stir in the 1 $^1/_2$ teaspoons lemon juice; let cool for about 4 minutes (glaze continues to thicken as it cools).

6 Invert cake pan onto a serving plate; carefully lift off pan to release cake. If any pears remain in pan, remove them and arrange in their original places atop cake. Drizzle cake with half the warm glaze; then sprinkle with hazelnuts and drizzle with remaining glaze.

makes 16 servings

per serving: 253 calories, 3 g protein, 42 g carbohydrates, 8 g total fat, 57 mg cholesterol, 199 mg sodium

chocolate soufflés

preparation time: 50 minutes

$2/3$ cup unsweetened cocoa powder

About $3/4$ cup granulated sugar

4 teaspoons cornstarch

1 teaspoon instant espresso or coffee powder

1 cup low-fat (2%) milk

2 ounces bittersweet or semisweet chocolate, finely chopped

2 teaspoons vanilla

7 large egg whites, at room temperature

$1/4$ teaspoon cream of tartar

$1/16$ to $1/8$ teaspoon salt

About 2 tablespoons powdered sugar

1 In a 1- to 2-quart pan, stir together cocoa, $1/4$ cup of the granulated sugar, cornstarch, and instant espresso. Whisk in milk. Cook over medium heat, whisking constantly, until mixture boils and thickens slightly (about 1 minute). Remove from heat and add chocolate and vanilla; whisk until chocolate is melted and mixture is smooth. Let cool completely.

2 While mixture cools, lightly grease six $1\frac{1}{2}$-cup custard cups; sprinkle each lightly with granulated sugar to coat bottom. Place cups in a large baking pan and set aside.

3 In a deep bowl, beat egg whites with an electric mixer on high speed until frothy. Add cream of tartar, salt, and $1/2$ cup of the granulated sugar, 1 tablespoon at a time; beat until whites hold firm, moist peaks. Stir about a third of the whites into cooled chocolate mixture; then fold chocolate mixture into remaining whites.

4 Gently fill custard cups equally with batter. Position oven rack in bottom third of a 350° oven; set baking pan on rack. Pour boiling water into pan around cups up to level of batter. Bake until soufflés are puffy and feel firm when gently pressed (about 25 minutes). Carefully lift cups from pan and sprinkle soufflés with powdered sugar. Serve immediately.

makes 6 servings

per serving: 238 calories, 8 g protein, 42 g carbohydrates, 7 g total fat, 3 mg cholesterol, 122 mg sodium

port ice

preparation time: 15 minutes
chilling and freezing time: about 5 hours

$1/2$ cup sugar

1 cup port or cream sherry

$1/4$ cup fresh orange juice

1 teaspoon aromatic bitters

1 In a 1- to 2-quart pan, combine sugar and $1\frac{1}{2}$ cups water. Bring to a boil over high heat, stirring until sugar is dissolved. Remove from heat and let cool; then stir in port, orange juice, and bitters. Cover and refrigerate until cold (about 1 hour). Pour port mixture into a metal pan 8 to 9 inches square; cover and freeze until solid (about 4 hours) or for up to 3 days.

2 To serve, break mixture into chunks with a heavy spoon, transfer to a blender or food processor, and whirl until slushy; then spoon into bowls and serve at once. (Or pour cold port mixture into container of a self-refrigerated ice cream machine and freeze according to manufacturer's instructions.)

makes 6 to 8 servings

per serving: 114 calories, 0.1 g protein, 19 g carbohydrates, 0 g total fat, 0 mg cholesterol, 3 mg sodium

amaretto soufflé

preparation time: 50 minutes

---

¹/₂ cup coarsely crushed amaretti cookies (about ten 11-inch cookies)

³/₄ cup low-fat (2%) milk

3 large egg yolks

6 tablespoons granulated sugar

¹/₄ cup all-purpose flour

¹/₄ cup almond-flavored or other nut-flavored liqueur

¹/₄ teaspoon almond extract

5 large egg whites

1 teaspoon cream of tartar

¹/₈ teaspoon salt

About 1 tablespoon sifted powdered sugar

1 Sprinkle crushed cookies over bottom of a greased 1¹/₂- to 1³/₄-quart soufflé dish. Place dish in a larger pan (at least 2 inches deep); set aside.

2 Bring milk to a boil in a medium-size nonstick pan over medium heat (about 5 minutes), stirring often. Remove from heat and let cool slightly.

3 In a large bowl, whisk egg yolks and 3 tablespoons of the granulated sugar until thick and lemon-colored. Add flour and whisk until smoothly blended. Whisk in a little of the warm milk, then whisk egg yolk mixture back into warm milk in pan. Return to heat and stir constantly (be careful not to scratch pan) just until mixture boils and thickens slightly. Return to large bowl and whisk in liqueur and almond extract; let cool completely.

4 In a clean large, deep bowl beat egg whites and 1 tablespoon water with an electric mixer on high speed until frothy. Beat in cream of tartar and salt. Then beat in remaining 3 tablespoons granulated sugar, 1 tablespoon at a time; continue to beat until mixture holds stiff, moist peaks. Stir about a third of the egg white mixture into yolk mixture; then fold all of yolk mixture into egg white mixture.

5 Gently spoon soufflé batter into prepared dish. Set pan with dish on middle rack of a 350° oven. Pour boiling water into larger pan up to level of soufflé batter. Bake until soufflé is richly browned and center jiggles only slightly when dish is gently shaken (about 25 minutes); if top begins to brown excessively, carefully cover dish with foil. As soon as soufflé is done, sprinkle it with powdered sugar and serve immediately.

makes 6 servings

per serving: 198 calories, 6 g protein, 29 g carbohydrates, 4 g total fat, 109 mg cholesterol, 115 mg sodium

STORING COFFEE: Heat and moisture cause coffee to go stale quickly, so store both beans and ground coffee airtight—preferably in glass jars with tight screw-on lids—in the refrigerator or freezer. When you want to brew coffee, just remove the amount you need; there's no need to thaw it or bring it to room temperature before using. Buy coffee in small quantities, since it loses its freshness after about a month even if stored properly.

mexican cocoa cake

preparation time: 40 to 50 minutes

Spiced Cream (optional; page 585)

1 cup sifted cake flour

¹/₃ cup unsweetened cocoa powder

1 teaspoon *each* baking soda, baking powder, and ground cinnamon

6 large egg whites

1¹/₃ cups firmly packed brown sugar

1 cup plain nonfat yogurt

2 teaspoons vanilla

¹/₄ teaspoon almond extract

Powdered sugar

1 Prepare Spiced Cream, if desired; refrigerate.

2 In a small bowl, mix flour, cocoa, baking soda, baking powder, and cinnamon. In a large bowl, beat egg whites, brown sugar, yogurt, vanilla, and almond extract until well blended. Stir in flour mixture and beat just until evenly moistened.

3 Pour batter into a square 8-inch nonstick (or greased regular) baking pan. Bake in a 350° oven until center of cake springs back when lightly pressed (30 to 40 minutes). Let cake cool in pan on a rack for 15 minutes; then invert it onto a serving plate. Serve warm or cool. If made ahead, wrap cooled cake airtight and store in a cool place until next day (freeze for longer storage).

4 Just before serving, sift powdered sugar over cake. To serve, cut cake into wedges or rectangles. If desired, sift more powdered sugar over each serving; then top with Spiced Cream, if desired.

makes 8 servings

per serving: 226 calories, 6 g protein, 51 g carbohydrates, 0.6 g total fat, 0.6 mg cholesterol, 297 mg sodium

campari ice

preparation time: 15 minutes
chilling & freezing time: about 5 hours

¹/₂ cup sugar

1 cup sweet vermouth or fresh orange juice

2 tablespoons Campari
or 2 teaspoons aromatic bitters

1 tablespoon lime juice

Thin lime slices

1 In a 1- to 2-quart pan, combine sugar and 1¹/₂ cups water. Bring to a boil over high heat, stirring until sugar is dissolved. Remove from heat and let cool; then stir in vermouth, Campari, and lime juice. Cover mixture and refrigerate until cold (about 1 hour).

2 Pour mixture into a metal pan 8 to 9 inches square; cover and freeze until solid (about 4 hours) or for up to 3 days.

3 To serve, break mixture into chunks with a heavy spoon, transfer to a blender or food processor, and whirl until slushy; then spoon into bowls and serve at once. (Or pour cold port mixture into container of a self-refrigerated ice cream machine and freeze according to manufacturer's instructions.) Garnish individual servings with lime slices.

makes 6 to 8 servings

per serving: 120 calories, 0 g protein, 20 g carbohydrates, 0 g total fat, 0 mg cholesterol, 4 mg sodium

oranges with rum syrup & spiced cream

preparation time: about 35 minutes
freezing and chilling time: 45 minutes to 1 hour

Spiced Cream (recipe follows)

$1/2$ cup sugar

1 $1/2$ cups water

2 teaspoons whole cloves

2 tablespoons light rum

4 large oranges (about 3 lbs. total)

1 Prepare Spiced Cream; refrigerate.

2 In a small pan, combine sugar, water, and cloves. Bring to a boil over high heat; then boil until reduced to $3/4$ cup (about 20 minutes). Remove from heat, stir in rum, and let cool. (At this point, you may cover and refrigerate for up to 5 days.)

3 With a sharp knife, cut peel and all white membrane from oranges. Slice fruit into 6 dessert bowls, dividing equally. Add rum syrup and Spiced Cream to taste.

makes 6 servings

SPICED CREAM

1 Pour $1/4$ cup nonfat milk into small bowl of an electric mixer. Cover bowl; then freeze mixer beaters and bowl of milk until milk is slushy (30 to 45 minutes). In a small pan, sprinkle $1/2$ teaspoon unflavored gelatin over $1/4$ cup cold water; let stand until gelatin is softened (about 3 minutes). Then stir mixture over low heat just until gelatin is dissolved. Remove from heat.

2 To slushy milk, add gelatin, $2/3$ cup instant nonfat dry milk, 2 tablespoons sugar, 1 teaspoon vanilla, and $1/2$ teaspoon ground cinnamon. Beat on high speed until mixture holds soft peaks (5 to 10 minutes). Cover and refrigerate for at least 15 minutes or for up to 2 days. If needed, whisk or beat again before serving until cream holds soft peaks. Serve cold.

makes about 2 cups

per serving of oranges: 153 calories, 1 g protein, 36 g carbohydrates, 0.4 g total fat, 0 mg cholesterol, 0.6 mg sodium

per tablespoon of spiced cream: 9 calories, 0.6 g protein, 2 g carbohydrates, 0 g total fat, 0.3 mg cholesterol, 9 mg sodium

oranges in ginger champagne

preparation time: about 15 minutes

$3/4$ cup *each* sugar and water

2 tablespoons minced candied ginger

4 medium-size oranges

1 bottle dry champagne or 4 cups ginger ale

1 In a 2- to 3-quart pan, combine sugar, water, and ginger. Cook over medium heat, stirring, until sugar is dissolved. Increase heat to high and boil, without stirring, for 5 minutes. Transfer to a bowl; cool, cover, and refrigerate until cold or until next day.

2 Peel oranges and remove white membrane. Holding oranges over bowl of ginger syrup, cut between segments to release fruit; stir. Cover and refrigerate for 3 hours.

3 Spoon orange mixture into champagne or wine glasses. Fill with champagne.

makes 8 servings

per serving: 188 calories, 0.7 g protein, 33 g carbohydrates, 0.2 g total fat, 0 mg cholesterol, 7 mg sodium

german chocolate cheesecake

preparation time: 30 minutes
cooking time: about 1 hour and 10 minutes
cooling and chilling time: at least 4 1/2 hours

1 cup chocolate graham cracker crumbs (about twelve square 2-inch crackers)

3 tablespoons apple jelly, melted and cooled slightly

3 large packages (about 8 oz. *each*) nonfat cream cheese, at room temperature

1 cup granulated sugar

3/4 cup unsweetened cocoa powder

1/3 cup all-purpose flour

1/3 cup semisweet chocolate chips, melted and cooled slightly

1/2 cup nonfat milk

2 large eggs

2 large egg whites

2 teaspoons vanilla

2/3 cup regular rolled oats

1/3 cup sweetened shredded coconut

1/4 cup finely chopped pecans

2/3 cup firmly packed brown sugar

3 tablespoons *each* half-and-half and light corn syrup

2 tablespoons butter or margarine

1. In a food processor or a large bowl, whirl or stir together graham cracker crumbs and jelly just until crumbs are evenly moistened. Press crumbs firmly over bottom of a 9-inch nonstick or regular cheesecake pan with a removable rim. Bake in a 350° oven until crust is slightly darker in color (about 15 minutes).

2. Meanwhile, in clean food processor or large bowl, combine cream cheese, granulated sugar, cocoa, flour, chocolate, milk, eggs, egg whites, and vanilla. Whirl or beat with an electric mixer until smooth.

3. Pour cream cheese filling over crust. Return to oven and bake until filling jiggles only slightly in center when pan is gently shaken (about 45 minutes). Remove pan from oven and run a slender knife between cheesecake and pan rim; let cheesecake cool in pan on a rack for 30 minutes.

4. Meanwhile, toast oats in a wide nonstick frying pan over medium heat for 5 minutes, stirring often. Add coconut and pecans; continue to cook, stirring often, until mixture is slightly darker in color (3 to 5 more minutes). Transfer oat mixture to a bowl and let cool. In same pan, combine brown sugar, half-and-half, corn syrup, and butter. Cook over medium heat, stirring, until butter is melted and mixture is smoothly blended. Stir in oat mixture. Remove pan from heat and let mixture cool for 5 minutes.

5. Gently spoon coconut topping over cheesecake; let cool completely. Then cover cooled cheesecake and refrigerate until cold (at least 4 hours) or until next day. Remove pan rim before serving.

makes 12 to 16 servings

per serving: 300 calories, 11 g protein, 51 g carbohydrates, 7 g total fat, 41 mg cholesterol, 326 mg sodium

apple & date betty

preparation time: 20 minutes
cooking time: 50 to 55 minutes

2 cups soft whole wheat bread crumbs

3 tablespoons butter or margarine, melted

1/4 cup firmly packed brown sugar

1/4 cup granulated sugar

1/2 teaspoon ground cinnamon

1/8 teaspoon ground nutmeg

4 cups peeled, sliced tart apples

1/2 cup coarsely chopped pitted dates

1 tablespoon lemon juice

1 In a medium-size bowl, lightly mix bread crumbs, butter, and brown sugar. Sprinkle half the mixture over bottom of a shallow 2-quart casserole; set aside remaining mixture.

2 In a large bowl, stir together granulated sugar, cinnamon, and nutmeg. Add apples and dates; mix gently to coat fruit with sugar mixture. Drizzle fruit mixture with lemon juice, then cover evenly over crumb mixture in casserole. Sprinkle with 2 tablespoons water; cover evenly with remaining crumb mixture.

3 Set casserole in a larger baking pan to catch any drips. Cover and bake in a 375° oven for 30 minutes. Then uncover and continue to bake until filling is bubbly in center, apples are very tender when pierced, and topping is crisp (20 to 25 more minutes). Serve hot or warm; to serve, spoon into bowls.

makes 6 servings

per serving: 242 calories, 2 g protein, 47 g carbohydrates, 7 g total fat, 16 mg cholesterol, 151 mg sodium

nectarine-blueberry cream pie

preparation time: 35 minutes, plus 15 minutes for filling to stand
cooking time: about 1 1/4 hours

Pie pastry

1 cup nonfat sour cream

1 teaspoon cornstarch

2 cups fresh blueberries

4 cups peeled, sliced firm-ripe nectarines

1 teaspoon vanilla

1/2 cup granulated sugar

3 tablespoons quick-cooking tapioca

1/2 cup firmly packed brown sugar

2/3 cup all-purpose flour

3 tablespoons butter or margarine, melted and cooled slightly

2 tablespoons smooth unsweetened applesauce

1 Prepare pie pastry and line pie pan, but do not prick pastry after lining pan. Bake pastry shell on lowest rack of a 425° oven until golden (12 to 15 minutes; pastry may puff, but filling will press it down again). Remove from oven and place on a rack. Reduce oven temperature to 350°.

2 While pastry is baking, in a large bowl, beat sour cream and cornstarch until smoothly blended. Stir in blueberries, nectarines, and vanilla. Stir together granulated sugar and tapioca; add to fruit mixture and mix gently. Let stand for 15 minutes to soften tapioca, stirring occasionally. Then pour filling into warm pastry shell and set aside.

3 In a small bowl, combine brown sugar, flour, butter, and apple-sauce. Stir until mixture is evenly moistened. With your fingers, squeeze mixture to form large lumps; then crumble evenly over filling.

4 Set pie pan in a larger baking pan to catch any drips. Bake pie on lowest oven rack until filling is bubbly in center and topping is well browned (about 1 hour); if crust or topping begins to darken excessively, cover it with foil. Let cool on a rack before serving; serve warm.

makes 8 to 10 servings

per serving: 390 calories, 6 g protein, 64 g carbohydrates, 13 g total fat, 10 mg cholesterol, 139 mg sodium

pumpkin cheesecake

preparation time: 25 minutes
cooking time: about 1 hour
cooling and chilling time: at least 4 1/2 hours

2/3 cup firmly packed brown sugar

3 tablespoons all-purpose flour

1/4 cup butter or margarine, melted

2 large packages (about 8 oz. *each*) nonfat cream cheese, at room temperature

1 can (about 1 lb.) pumpkin

2 large eggs

3/4 cup granulated sugar

2 tablespoons all-purpose flour

1 teaspoon ground cinnamon

1 teaspoon vanilla

1/4 teaspoon *each* ground ginger and ground nutmeg

1 cup nonfat sour cream

1 tablespoon granulated sugar

1/2 cup coarsely crushed gingersnaps (about nine 2-inch cookies)

1 In a food processor or a large bowl, whirl or stir together the 2 cups finely crushed gingersnaps, brown sugar, and the 3 tablespoons flour. Add butter; whirl or rub with your fingers until mixture resembles coarse crumbs. Press crumb mixture firmly over bottom and 1/2 inch up sides of a 9-inch nonstick or regular cheesecake pan with a removable rim. Bake in a 350° oven until crust smells toasted and feels slightly firmer in center when gently pressed (about 10 minutes).

2 Meanwhile, in clean food processor or large bowl, combine cream cheese, pumpkin, eggs, the 3/4 cup granulated sugar, the 2 tablespoons flour, cinnamon, vanilla, ginger, and nutmeg. Whirl or beat with an electric mixer until smooth.

3 Pour cream cheese filling into baked crust. Return to oven and bake until filling jiggles only slightly in center when pan is gently shaken (about 50 minutes). Let cool in pan on a rack for 30 minutes. Meanwhile, in a small bowl, gently stir together sour cream and the 1 tablespoon sugar; cover and refrigerate.

4 Spread cooled cheesecake with sour cream topping. Cover and refrigerate until cold (at least 4 hours) or until next day. Just before serving, remove pan rim; sprinkle cheesecake with the 1/2 cup coarsely crushed gingersnaps.

makes 12 servings

per serving: 317 calories, 10 g protein, 54 g carbohydrates, 7 g total fat, 50 mg cholesterol, 404 mg sodium

anise poofs

preparation time: about 35 minutes
standing time: 8 to 24 hours

About 2 cups sifted powdered sugar

1 cup all-purpose flour

1 teaspoon baking powder

1/4 teaspoon ground cinnamon

1 tablespoon olive oil

1 large egg, beaten

2 tablespoons anisette liqueur; or 1 teaspoon anise extract (or to taste) blended with 5 teaspoons water

1 teaspoon vanilla

1 In a large bowl, stir together 2 cups of the powdered sugar, flour, baking powder, and cinnamon. Add oil, egg, liqueur, and vanilla; stir until well blended. Turn dough out onto a board lightly dusted with powdered sugar; knead until smooth, about 4 turns.

2 Cut dough into 6 pieces. Roll each piece into a rope 20 inches long and about 1/2 inch wide.

3 Cut each rope into 2-inch lengths. Place pieces about 1 1/2 inches apart on lightly oiled large baking sheets. Let cookies stand, uncovered, for 8 to 24 hours. (Do not omit standing time; if dough does not stand, cookies will not puff.) Then bake in a 325° oven until pale golden (about 8 minutes). Immediately transfer cookies to racks and let cool.

makes 5 dozen cookies

per cookie: 27 calories, 0.3 g protein, 5 g carbohydrates, 0.5 g total fat, 4 mg cholesterol, 9 mg sodium

lime cheesecake

preparation time: 20 minutes
cooking time: 45 to 55 minutes
cooling and chilling time: at least 4 ½ hours

1 ½ cups graham cracker crumbs (about
   eighteen square 2-inch crackers)

1 cup plus 1 tablespoon sugar

¼ cup butter or margarine,
   at room temperature

2 large packages (about 8 oz. *each*) nonfat
   cream cheese, at room temperature

2 cups nonfat sour cream

2 large eggs

2 large egg whites

1 tablespoon grated lime peel

¼ cup lime juice

3 tablespoons all-purpose flour

Lime slices

1 In a food processor or a large bowl, whirl or stir together graham cracker crumbs, 2 tablespoons of the sugar, and butter until mixture resembles coarse crumbs. Press mixture firmly over bottom and ½ inch up sides of a 9-inch nonstick or regular cheesecake pan with a removable rim. Bake in a 350° oven until lightly browned (about 10 minutes).

2 Meanwhile, in clean food processor or large bowl, combine ¾ cup plus 2 tablespoons of the sugar, cream cheese, 1 cup of the sour cream, eggs, egg whites, lime peel, lime juice, and flour. Whirl or beat with an electric mixer until smooth.

3 Pour cream cheese filling into crust. Return to oven and bake until filling jiggles only slightly in center when pan is gently shaken (35 to 45 minutes). Let cool in pan on a rack for 30 minutes. Meanwhile, in a small bowl, gently stir together remaining 1 cup sour cream and remaining 1 tablespoon sugar; cover and refrigerate.

4 Spread cooled cheesecake with sour cream topping. Cover and refrigerate until cold (at least 4 hours) or until next day. Before serving, remove pan rim and garnish cheesecake with lime slices.

makes 12 to 16 servings

per serving: 211 calories, 9 g protein, 31 g carbohydrates, 5 g total fat, 43 mg cholesterol, 305 mg sodium

peach cobbler with almond topping

preparation time: 35 minutes, plus 15 minutes for filling to stand
cooking time: about 1 hour

1 cup almond paste

½ cup sugar

¼ cup cornstarch

9 medium-size firm-ripe peaches

2 tablespoons sugar

2 tablespoons lemon juice

1 Crumble almond paste into a medium-size bowl. Add the ½ cup sugar and 2 tablespoons of the corn starch. Rub together with your fingers until well blended. With your fingers, squeeze mixture to form large lumps; set aside.

2 Peel and pit peaches; then slice them into a shallow 1½- to 2-quart casserole. Add the 2 tablespoons sugar, lemon juice, and remaining 2 tablespoons cornstarch; mix gently. Spread out fruit mixture in an even layer; then crumble almond topping over top.

3 Set casserole in a larger baking pan to catch any drips. Bake in a 350° oven until fruit mixture is bubbly in center and topping is browned (45 to 50 minutes); if topping begins to darken excessively, cover it with foil. Let cool slightly; spoon into bowls.

makes 6 to 8 servings

per serving: 277 calories, 4 g protein, 51 g carbohydrates, 8 g total fat, 0 mg cholesterol, 4 mg sodium

amaretto cheesecake

preparation time: 20 minutes
cooking time: about 1 1/2 hours
Cooling and chilling time: at least 4 1/2 hours

2 cups graham cracker crumbs

1/4 cup butter or margarine, melted

1/4 teaspoon almond extract

2 tablespoons slivered almonds

4 large packages (about 8 oz *each*) nonfat
   cream cheese, at room temperature

1 cup granulated sugar

3 large eggs

2 large egg whites

1 cup nonfat sour cream

2 tablespoons almond-flavored liqueur

2/3 cup firmly packed brown sugar

3 tablespoons each half-and-half
   and light corn syrup

2 tablespoons butter or margarine

1 teaspoon almond-flavored liqueur, or to taste

1 In a food processor or a large bowl, whirl or stir together graham cracker crumbs, the 1/4 cup melted butter, and almond extract just until crumbs are evenly moistened. Press crumbs firmly over bottom of a 9-inch nonstick or regular cheesecake pan with a removable rim. Bake in a 350° oven until crust is slightly darker in color (about 15 minutes).

2 Meanwhile, toast almonds in a small frying pan over medium heat until golden (3 to 5 minutes), stirring often. Transfer almonds to a bowl and set aside. In clean food processor or large bowl, combine cream cheese, granulated sugar, eggs, egg whites, sour cream, and the 2 tablespoons liqueur. Whirl or beat with an electric mixer until smooth.

3 Pour cream cheese filling over baked crust. Return to oven and bake until filling jiggles only slightly in center when pan is gently shaken (about 1 hour and 5 minutes). Let cheesecake cool in pan on a rack for 30 minutes.

4 Meanwhile, in a 1- to 1 1/2-quart pan, combine brown sugar, half-and-half, corn syrup, and the 2 tablespoons butter. Bring mixture just to a boil over medium heat, stirring constantly. Remove pan from heat and let cool for about 4 minutes; glaze thickens as it cools. Stir in the 1 teaspoon liqueur; set aside.

5 Run a slender knife between cheesecake and pan rim, then remove pan rim. Stir glaze and drizzle over cheesecake; let cool completely. Then lightly cover cooled cheesecake and refrigerate until cold (at least 4 hours) or until next day.

makes 12 to 16 servings

per serving: 321 calories, 14 g protein, 47 g carbohydrates, 8 g total fat, 67 mg cholesterol, 505 mg sodium

apricot slims

preparation time: 15 minutes
chilling time: at least 30 minutes

1 package (about 6 oz.) dried apricots

4 cup sweetened shredded or flaked coconut

1 tablespoon orange juice

2 tablespoons finely chopped almonds

3 tablespoons powdered sugar

1 In a food processor, combine apricots, coconut, and orange juice. Whirl until mixture begins to hold together in a ball.

2 Divide apricot mixture into 4 equal portions and wrap each in plastic wrap. Refrigerate until cold (at least 30 minutes).

3 In a small bowl, mix almonds and powdered sugar. Sprinkle a fourth of the almond mixture on a board. Place one portion of the apricot mixture atop almond mixture; roll apricot mixture back and forth with your palms to form a 16-inch rope. Repeat to make 3 more ropes, using remaining almond and apricot mixtures. To serve, cut ropes diagonally into 2-inch pieces.

makes 32 pieces

per piece: 20 calories, 0.3 g protein, 4 g carbohydrates, 0.3 g total fat, 0 mg cholesterol, 2 mg sodium

index